PRAISE FOR "FILI

'David Wood has written a wonderfully evocative insider's view of the shooting of one of the best British films ever made.'

Sir Alan Parker

'I adored *If….*, and remember you all so vividly. I saw it sitting in the dark cinema beside an ex-public schoolboy: he drew in his breath sharply when it started, and muttered, "That's exactly how it was." I remember clearly exact moments and scenes, as if I have just seen them again. What a brilliant thing you have done, recalling what it was like being directed by the great Lindsay Anderson, and being part of this hugely important film and its dazzling cast.'

Joanna Lumley OBE

'*If….* is a classic movie – I was at the première in 1968 and we all sensed it then. Having read David Wood's wonderfully evocative account of its making, I've a feeling this book's going to be something of a classic, too.'

Gyles Brandreth

Holly -
All good wishes
David Wood

FILMING if....

DAVID WOOD

The Book Guild Ltd

First published in Great Britain in 2018 by
The Book Guild Ltd
9 Priory Business Park
Wistow Road, Kibworth
Leicestershire, LE8 0RX
Freephone: 0800 999 2982
www.bookguild.co.uk
Email: info@bookguild.co.uk
Twitter: @bookguild

Typeset in Adobe Garamond Pro

Printed and bound in Great Britain by CPI Group (UK) Ltd, Croydon, CR0 4YY

ISBN 978 1912362 592

British Library Cataloguing in Publication Data.
A catalogue record for this book is available from the British Library.

For Jacqui, Katherine and Rebecca.

CONTENTS

AUTHOR'S NOTE

In the late '60s, as a young actor cutting his professional teeth in repertory theatre, to be cast in a film was a major excitement. I had never worked in front of a camera before, but the name of the director – Lindsay Anderson – was very familiar to me, mainly from his theatre work. Filming with Lindsay was exhilarating, an education. And I think all of us knew we were involved in something rather special. Nearly fifty years on, I have tried in these pages to give a flavour of what the acting experience was like, the day-to-day challenges and the sheer pleasure of working with a man I consider to be an often underrated genius of the cinema.

My thanks to Malcolm McDowell for his warm Foreword, to George Perry for remembering Lindsay Anderson the man, his career and his importance in the history of British cinema, and to Christie Hickman for her sympathetic and skilled editing of my memories. Thanks, too, to the Lindsay Anderson Foundation, whose members encouraged me to write this book. The Foundation makes every effort to keep Lindsay's name and work alive and revered. More information at www.lindsayanderson.com.

DW

FOREWORD

by Malcolm McDowell

In 1968, Lindsay Anderson and writer David Sherwin's film *If....* plunged a dagger into the heart of the British Establishment.

To use a public school as a metaphor for the state of the nation was, at the time, a master stroke. By 1968, Britain was slowly emerging from a post-war malaise. Against a background of the Vietnam war and the Paris riots, rebellion was in the air. Young people wanted to be heard and this film gave them a voice.

David Wood's account of the shooting of the film brings back lots of wonderful memories for me. Of course, my memories are slightly different, but I remember the great camaraderie between the three rebels – myself, David and Richard Warwick. For all three of us, this experience was life-changing. Meeting and then working with the great director, Lindsay Anderson, made a deep impression on all the young actors in the film. My relationship with Lindsay went on until his death and he became a mentor and a great influence in my life.

David's memoir captures beautifully some of the day to day shooting of the film and the relationship of all the actors and production people involved. He had a unique opportunity to observe Lindsay at work and how his beautiful direction was so poetic. Yet none of us could have predicted that this iconoclastic film would become such a hit with the general public.

David went on to be a wonderful writer, actor and director… quite the Renaissance man. Richard Warwick, a wonderful, warm human being, sadly passed away when he was far too young. Stanley Kubrick saw *If*…. and cast me in *A Clockwork Orange.*

Although David and I haven't seen much of each other in the fifty years since the making of the film, we are forever tied by the bond that is *If*…. And we will always be brothers.

Malcolm McDowell, Ojai, California

INTRODUCTION

I caught the acting bug very early on, mainly perhaps, through being taken to see *Peter Pan* at the Scala Theatre each Christmas for three years from the age of five. My parents offered me the chance to see other festive productions, but, having experienced JM Barrie's classic once, I was (forgive the pun) hooked, and insisted on returning to the wonders of Neverland. I loved the flying, Nana the dog and the creation of Wendy's house, but just as exciting was the theatricality of the lights going down, the music striking up, and the curtain rising.

We lived in Banstead, Surrey. My mother and father enjoyed ballroom dancing, won several cups locally, and for a time ran a dancing school. Music featured strongly in the house, of the popular variety. My father, who had entertained in an amateur concert party during the war, encouraged me to sing songs, accompanied by him at the piano. *Blue for a Boy*, from a current West End musical, was a favourite. I started piano lessons, joined the church choir and first trod the boards aged eight in a Sunday School play about the Catechism. For some reason I felt totally at home on the stage of the Banstead Institute Hall. And when we acquired a television in time to watch the Coronation in 1953, I was entranced by variety shows and a children's magazine programme called *Whirligig*, which featured piano-playing, puppetry and conjuring, all of which led me towards the idea of entertaining. Indeed, 25 years later, when I created a touring children's theatre company, I called it *Whirligig Theatre*.

As an only child, conjuring was the perfect hobby. My mother took me to Hamleys and bought me some tricks. My Auntie Connie gave me a book called *The Boys' Book of Conjuring*. When I was ten, my mother made the curtains for a toy theatre fashioned from an orange box, and I wrote and produced puppet plays. A few years later, by which time we had moved to the South coast, I started performing magic at children's parties. School plays, talent competitions, amateur dramatic society performances and residential summer drama courses led to me wanting to go to drama school, but my sensible headmaster at Chichester High School for Boys persuaded me to try for university. An attempt to do French and Drama at Bristol University failed, but I managed to gain a place at Worcester College, Oxford, which somewhat surprisingly proved to be a very effective way of eventually entering the theatrical profession.

In my first year I played in and wrote songs for *Hang Down Your Head and Die*, the Experimental Theatre Club production about capital punishment, directed by Braham Murray, which incredibly transferred to the Comedy Theatre, London and gained me a Best Newcomer nomination in the Variety Critics' Poll.

The following year I was in Michael Rudman's Oxford Theatre Group production of *A Spring Song* on the Edinburgh Fringe, which transferred to the Mermaid Theatre. Having also cut my teeth in revue with Michael Palin and Diana Quick, and having played Algernon in *The Importance of Being Earnest* and the Fool in *King Lear* for the Oxford University Dramatic Society, I was cast as Wagner, Faustus' servant, in the widely publicised Richard Burton and Elizabeth Taylor production of *Doctor Faustus* at the Oxford Playhouse. This led to my girlfriend, Sheila Dawson, who understudied Elizabeth Taylor's Helen of Troy, and I being given rides in the Burtons' Rolls and to Miss Taylor kissing me on the lips as midnight struck to herald my twenty-second birthday.

Looking back, I couldn't have had a better start. The Mermaid adventure had even given me an Equity card, without having had to achieve the obligatory forty weeks in rep. The fact that I managed to scrape through with a third class degree was nothing short of a miracle. I had spent far more time working on my theatrical activities than my academic studies. Yet my tutor, the esteemed Christopher Ricks, seemed to indulge, even encourage, my performing ambitions. He even paid me to give magic entertainments at his children's birthday parties.

Within days of graduating in 1966, I was in rehearsal for *Four Degrees Over*, a musical revue I co-wrote with composer John Gould. The cast of four comprised John, Adèle Weston (later to become Adèle Geras, successful children's writer), Bob (later Sir Bob) Scott and myself. We rehearsed, courtesy of Sir Bernard Miles, in the Mermaid Theatre rehearsal room, before touring, on our way to the Edinburgh Festival Fringe. We opened at the King's Lynn Festival on the very afternoon that England's football team won the World Cup. We even gave the audience regular score updates. Next day we performed at the Mermaid, received two glowing reviews, and before even reaching Edinburgh, found ourselves with a West End transfer offer from producer Michael Codron. We were thrilled to open at the Fortune Theatre, the location of iconic revues like *Beyond The Fringe, Wait a Minim* and Flanders and Swann's *At the Drop of a Hat.* We didn't exactly set the West End alight, but we ran for several months and our cast album was produced on Parlophone by the legendary George Martin. It was almost unheard of to start one's professional career in the West End, so we were very fortunate.

Theatre In Education at Watford followed, based at the Palace Theatre. Recreating the story of *The Tay Bridge Disaster* in schools excited me. We were introducing theatre to children, most of whom had never experienced it before. We performed in the round, at very close quarters, to a volatile and sometimes cynical audience. But I was undaunted, unlike the actress who disappeared after the first performance and never came back. Later that year, after playing in a somewhat surreal production of Jarry's *Ubu Unchained* for the Traverse Theatre on the 1967 Edinburgh Festival fringe, featuring a splendid Miriam Margoyles wearing a kind of mattress designed by Gerald Scarfe, I was invited back to Watford to give my Wishee Washee in *Aladdin* for the Christmas season in the main theatre. Written by Michael Palin and Terry Jones pre-Monty Python, and featuring Amanda Barrie in the title role, the cast included Maureen Lipman as a hippie Genie of the Lamp, hopping around on a pogo stick.

As Wishee Washee I had most of the audience participation, and found that my magic shows had helped teach me to engage and control an audience of young people, who react en masse very differently from a couple of children in a room. I had a ball.

Then I was lucky enough to be invited to work as actor/ director for the new repertory company based at the Swan Theatre, Worcester. I directed *The Knack* and acted in *Next Time I'll Sing to You*, and, thanks to the artistic director, John Hole, performed in and directed Saturday morning children's theatre, which led to him inviting me to write the Christmas production. This was *The Tinderbox*, adapted from Hans Andersen, which I was never able to see, because of my panto commitment in Watford. But it led to me writing about seventy-five more plays for children over the next fifty years and being dubbed 'the national children's dramatist' by Irving Wardle in *The Times*.

The invitation to audition for *If....* came as I started work on another Worcester rep season, again directing and acting, plus planning another play for Christmas 1968. This turned out to be *The Owl and the Pussycat Went to See...*, the musical adaptation of Edward Lear I co-wrote with my then wife, Sheila Ruskin. The following year I directed it in London. Its success led to more productions in the regions, and really set the seal on my children's playwriting – and directing – future.

If.... became the cherry on a splendidly rich cake, and set me up for a satisfying and rewarding acting career, alongside my children's theatre activities, for the next two decades. I was fortunate enough to play opposite Sir Michael Redgrave in John Mortimer's *A Voyage Round My Father*, opposite Shelley Winters in a television play called *The Vamp*, and to play alongside Malcolm McDowell again in Jack Gold's film *Aces High*. But nothing eclipsed the excitement, novelty and prestige of being part of Lindsay Anderson's masterpiece. For this I have always been mightily grateful.

David Wood
2018

1

Crusaders

'I've split my trousers!' were the first pathetic words I blurted out to the legendary Lindsay Anderson. We were on stage at the Garrick Theatre in Charing Cross Road, on the set of the Brian Rix farce *Let Sleeping Wives Lie*, complete with what I remember as a circular bed. This was the unlikely setting for the auditions for Anderson's film *Crusaders*. He was interviewing a large number of 'boys' in their late teens and early twenties, some of whom were already professional actors and others who had replied to a series of advertisements in the classified columns of *The Times*. The film was to be set in an English public school.

Earlier that morning I had caught the first train from Worcester, where I was enjoying my second professional season of rep. Determined not to bask in the luxury of knowing I was in paid work for several months, and believing that the theatre was a business like any other, I had made it a rule to write five letters every day to prospective theatre directors, television producers and film casting directors, in the hope that one letter might lead to the next job. Methodically working through *Contacts*, the actors' bible, crammed with lists of useful addresses, I sent off thirty-five hand-written letters every week, plus duplicated CV and photo. The invitation to audition for *Crusaders* came from Miriam Brickman, at that time just one of the names on the list. Later I found out she was already the doyenne of film casting directors.

The audition was on a rehearsal day for our production of *Little Malcolm and his Struggle Against the Eunuchs*. There were only five in the cast and the rehearsal period was only two weeks. But Sam Walters, the director, kindly gave me the day off to make the trip to London.

Running enthusiastically up the steps from the tube, I tripped and split my trousers on one leg from the knee to the seat. Hence my embarrassed announcement to Lindsay. He was amused but unconcerned, and gave me a scene to read with several other auditionees. We sat in a semi circle, and read the scene a few times, swapping roles around. No comments were made. We were thanked for coming and stood up to leave. A friendly man, who I later discovered was called Neville Thompson, approached and asked what time train I was catching back to Worcester. Realising I had a couple of hours to kill, he asked if I would like to stay on and help by reading with another group. Somebody, it seemed, hadn't turned up, and they were one short. Without any thought that they might be interested in me, I ended up reading with several groups, totally relaxing in the process. Between the readings, Lindsay casually came over and talked to me. Among the general chat about my time as a student at Oxford, he suddenly asked what I understood by the term 'epic'. I managed to improvise a rambling reply about epic poems, and I think I might have even come up with an uninformed comment about Brecht.

Eventually, Neville thanked me for my time and I set off for Paddington, having enjoyed the morning, but with no clue as to whether or not I had met with approval. The scenes we had read gave little away as to the content of the film, but it was clear that a group of boys were rebelling against the public school system.

Although I hadn't attended a public school, certain elements of it were familiar to me, because I had been a day boy at a prep school attended by several boarders. So, at arm's length, as it were, I knew about dormitories, matrons, the prefect system, bullying and the importance of tradition and ritual. I also knew that Lindsay had a reputation as an unconventional and 'angry' director, so it was fairly certain the film would be somewhat controversial.

Back in Worcester, before the evening performance of a play called *Doctor Knock*, I was chatting to fellow actor Geoffrey Beevers, who asked me where I had been during the day. To my amazement, he told me that he knew about *Crusaders*, because he had been at Tonbridge School with the two writers of the original story and screenplay, John Howlett and David Sherwin. Geoffrey had been a prefect, and was fairly certain he had been used as a character in the story. I fancied Geoffrey was a little put out that he had not been invited to audition. This, I thought, might be because he was now a little old to play a schoolboy. Then it occurred to me that I was twenty-four! Maybe even I was too old.

A few days later I received a message asking if I would be willing to model the proposed school uniform in London. Not sure what this might involve, and wondering why they couldn't have asked somebody who lived in London, I decided it would be foolish to say no, particularly as they had thoughtfully scheduled it for a Sunday, when I would be free from acting or rehearsing. D'Arblay Street in Soho was the location. I descended to a small basement studio, where Lindsay and others were waiting.

To my surprise I found I was the only 'boy' there. Without the pressure of having to audition, I suppose I relaxed and enjoyed myself, never once suspecting that this exercise was in fact a kind of screen test. The uniform was based on the Eton model, a tailcoat and waistcoat, with the kind of trousers that might be worn at a wedding as part of a morning suit. Grey with stripes. There was a choice, so I went for those with the tightest legs, which I suppose I thought were more trendy than the wider, roomier variety. Come to think of it, this penchant for wearing tight trousers in real life probably led to me splitting the ones I wore to the audition. Later, during filming of the mock-fight on Cheltenham High Street, it happened again, this time to my school trousers. As I roll on the pavement a large expanse of white thigh can be seen where the seam of one leg has torn apart. Don't blink or you'll miss it. A strip of gaffer tape held it together for the succeeding takes.

I was told that one of the tests they were carrying out was a colour test on the proposed school tie. This proved to be black with a red, white and blue stripe. At the time I had no idea that *Crusaders* was using a public school as a metaphor for the state of Great Britain, so that the use of red, white and blue was of symbolic importance.

After posing for a few shots under simple lighting, Lindsay casually suggested that this rather boring task might be enlivened if I looked at the camera as though I hated it. Several other emotions were suggested, but again, I never got the impression that I was being tested. It was all very relaxed and enjoyable. Nothing much was said about the film itself, and as I headed back to Paddington to catch the Worcester train, I still had no idea that Lindsay might be interested in me. Looking back I can see this was a bit naïve, but I had never been up for a feature film before, so was totally green, and pleased to help out.

Back at the Swan Theatre, Worcester, *Little Malcolm* opened successfully, and rehearsals started for another play. News came through that I had definitely been offered a part in *Crusaders*. This was exciting enough. But even more intriguing was the invitation to go back to London for another audition, this time for a more important role. Eagerly, I asked if I could have permission to take another day trip to London, but this time, quite reasonably, the answer was no. We had too much work preparing for the next production. I rang my agent and asked her to pass on the news with my apologies. I hoped very much that Lindsay Anderson wouldn't think that my non-attendance at the audition signified

My school tie

a lack of interest in the project. I kept thinking that a call from the agent to Miriam Brickman's office wasn't enough. I needed to personally apologise and explain the reason why I couldn't leave Worcester. Somehow, I can't remember how, I managed to get hold of Lindsay's home number. I remember it involved ringing several people, stuffing coins into the pay phone in a glorified cupboard by the stage door. But eventually I had the number and dialled it. To my amazement, Lindsay answered it and graciously listened to my wittering. He said that another audition might not make much difference anyway and that I wasn't to worry.

Another week or so went by. News came through from my agent. I was asked when I could go to London to meet Lindsay and some other people to have a chat. A suitable time was found and I attended an enjoyable lunch with two actors, Malcolm McDowell and Richard Warwick, plus Lindsay and some production people.

Malcolm was immediately friendly, confident and quite extrovert. He was a few months older than me. We were both twenty-four. His craggy face was dominated by the most piercingly blue eyes. Having been to, in his words, 'a minor public school', he trained in acting at the London Academy of Music and Drama. I was impressed that he had worked for the Royal Shakespeare Company, though he admitted he had done little more than extra work. But he had recently played a small role in a film. I learned this was Nell Dunn's *Poor Cow*, directed by Kenneth Loach. Malcolm laughingly bragged that he had arrived on set and straight away performed nude in a bed scene with the star, Carol White. Later he found out the scene had been cut from the final edit.

Richard was much quieter than Malcolm, but it was easy to warm to this gentle, easy-going man, whose handsome face boasted the most wonderful smile. A year younger than me, he had been educated at a private school, then trained at the Royal Academy of Dramatic Art. He had already played a few stage roles, and modestly told me he had, the previous year, played Gregory in Franco Zefferelli's well-received film *Romeo and Juliet.*

The three of us seemed to click straight away. I was as amused by Malcolm's ebullience as I was charmed by Richard's endearing lack of pomposity. Quite what they made of me I cannot say. I was untrained, with no film experience, but I think my university acting and current work in rep helped me hold my own in our initial conversations. Over lunch, Lindsay spoke to us about *Crusaders.* Some of the conversation meant little to me because, I discovered later, both Malcolm and Richard had received a script and read it before the meeting. Not having had this advantage, I tried to answer questions intelligently, without really knowing what I was talking about.

I should have simply asked if I should have been sent a script, but at first I felt reticent to interrupt, and eventually felt it was too late to say anything. Lindsay asked us to start looking for pictures in magazines and newspapers, things which we might like to pin up in our studies. I wasn't quite sure whether we were simply to look for things that we as individuals liked, or whether we should be thinking of what our characters might like. As I didn't know my character, I felt more than a bit in the dark. All I managed to glean was the fact that my character's name was Johnny. Back in Worcester, waiting in the wings before the evening performance, I met Geoffrey Beevers again and told him I was playing Johnny. He reacted kindly and enthusiastically, saying that this was a major role. He was sure of it, because one of the two writers was called John, and he suspected that the character was based on him. This was exciting news and I finally plucked up the courage to ask if I had been meant to receive a script. Indeed I had, and, with an apology, it arrived soon after.

All became clear. Malcolm, Richard and I were playing the three rebellious schoolboys, who take on the Establishment figures, represented as much by the Prefects as the schoolmasters. In fact, the House Master leaves matters of school discipline entirely to the often sadistic Prefects. But the Headmaster represents the top of the traditional hierarchy and our three characters end up ritualistically shooting him from the school chapel roof.

The script was uncompromisingly critical of many aspects of the public school system and, consequently, critical of aspects of the British way of life. On a first reading, it was clear to me that some scenes were satirical rather than realistic in tone, yet the progression towards the chaos of the ending felt entirely plausible. If certain scenes were fantasy, they were written as though they were real, albeit occasionally surreal. From a personal point of view, I immediately related to Johnny, who seemed to be the most sensitive of the three rebels. Although I had never shown rebellious qualities as a teenager, I had certainly developed a keen awareness of injustice, and the behaviour of the Prefects in the *Crusaders* script made me instinctively want to foil them rather than to join them. I warmed to Johnny, who seemed to me to be not a natural leader, but a very good and faithful follower, happy to be led by Malcolm McDowell's Mick.

By the time the second draft of the script arrived, the title had been changed, thanks, apparently, to a suggestion made by Lindsay's friend Daphne Hunter who had been secretary to the magazine *Sight and Sound*, for whom Lindsay wrote film reviews. The new title, recalling Kipling's poem, and also suggesting a hypothetical possibility, was *If*.... To be accurate, there were only three dots following the word '*If*' on the title page. Many years later, I learned that Lindsay was always insistent on there being four dots. Interestingly, some publications have used only three, for instance the Sphere Books paperback of David Sherwin's story, which, although it has four dots inside, has only three on the cover! Also, the Paramount Pictures edition of the script only has three, although the Lorimer Publishing version in their *Modern Film Scripts* edition, has four throughout.

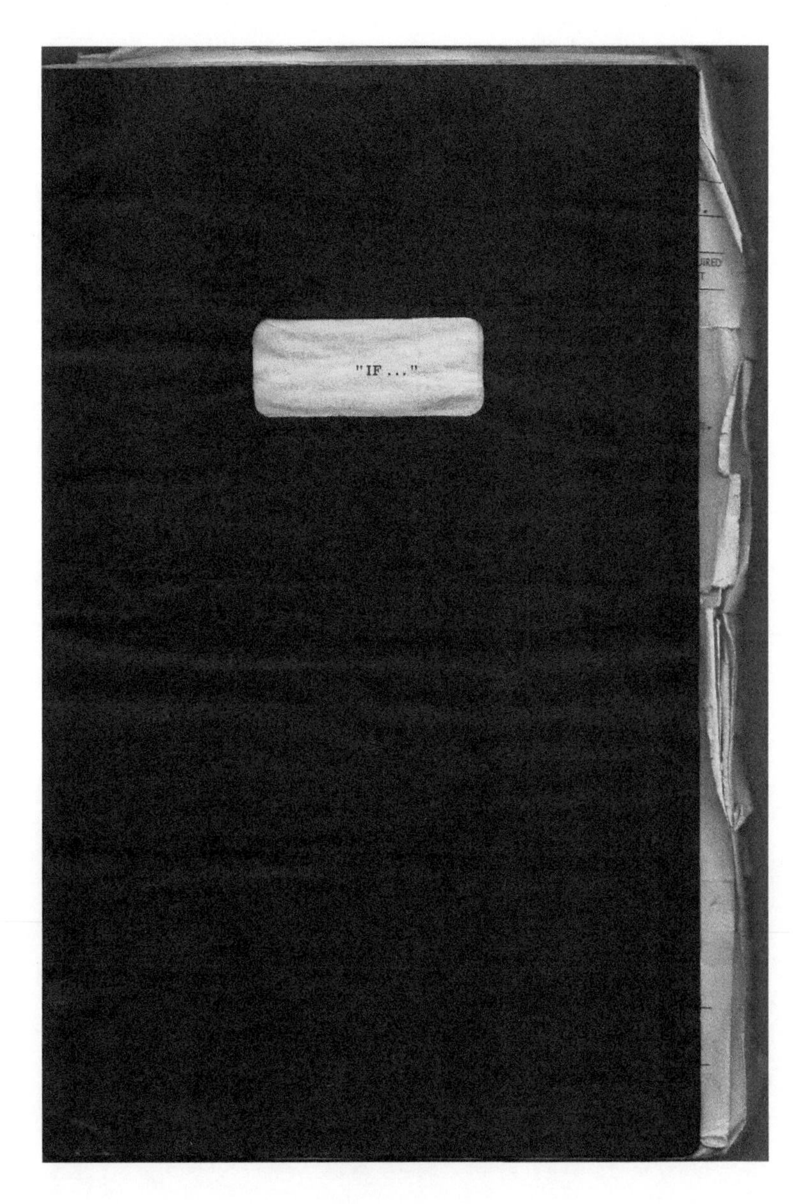

My official script

... BASIS

Form of Engagement for Artists Engaged in Films

APPROVED BY THE BRITISH FILM PRODUCERS ASSOCIATION AND THE BRITISH ACTORS' EQUITY ASSOCIATION

An Agreement made the twentieth day of February One thousand nine hundred and sixty eight BETWEEN Memorial Enterprises Ltd., 40 Piccadilly, London, W.1.

(hereinafter called "The Company") of the one part and David Wood c/o Noel Gay Artists, 24 Denmark Street, London, W.C.2.

(hereinafter called "The Artist") of the other part

whereby it is agreed as follows:—

SECTION 1.

The B.F.P.A. Equity Agreement. This Agreement shall incorporate the terms of the Agreement made between the British Film Producers Association and the British Actors' Equity Association and dated the Fifth day of December, 1947 (hereinafter called "the B.F.P.A. Equity Agreement") so far as the same are applicable hereto and this Engagement shall not contain any terms or provisions additional to those herein except as provided in Clause 5 of the B.F.P.A. Equity Agreement.

SECTION 2.

Engagement. The Company hereby engages the Artist and the Artist hereby accepts the engagement to perform the part of Johnny in a film entitled If and the engagement shall continue until the Company has completed the Artist's part in the production of the film.

SECTION 3. See note overleaf.

Daily Salary. Save as otherwise provided in this Agreement the Company shall pay to the Artist the sum of (£) per day (hereinafter called "the daily salary") for each day (or subject to the provisions of Clause 15 of the B.F.P.A. Equity Agreement, for each night) on which the Artist attends, following a call by the Company, to render services in the photographing or recording of the Artist's part in the film.

SECTION 4.

Guaranteed Period. The Company shall have first call on the Artist's services for a period of eight weeks (hereinafter called "the guaranteed period") commencing on the first day on which the Artist shall, following a call by the Company, attend to render services in the photographing or recording of the Artist's part, such day being on or about the fourteenth day of March 1968 that is to say not earlier than seven days before such date or failing such call, on the seventh day after such date.

SECTION 5.

Guaranteed Sum. In respect of the Artist's services during the guaranteed period the Company shall pay to the Artist not less than Six hundred and forty pounds*-------- (£640------------) (hereinafter called "the guaranteed sum"). The guaranteed sum shall include payments to the Artist under Clause 9 of the B.F.P.A. Equity Agreement and shall exclude payments to the Artist under Clause 10 of the B.F.P.A. Equity Agreement.
*eight weeks at £80 (eighty pounds) per week.

SECTION 6.

Half Salary.
(a) The Company shall pay to the Artist a sum equal to one-half of the daily salary in the circumstances provided for in Clauses 9 and 10 of the B.F.P.A. Equity Agreement.
(b) The Artist shall not be entitled to more than the daily salary on any day under this section and section 3 hereof, except when the Artist is paid for night work under the provisions of Clause 15 of the B.F.P.A. Equity Agreement.

SECTION 7.

Extending First Call. The Company may retain the first call on the Artist after the guaranteed period subject to the provisions of Clause 7 of the B.F.P.A. Equity Agreement.

continued over

My contract

SECTION 8.

Artist's Warranties.

The Artist warrants that

Delete words which do not apply and initial

(a) The Artist is and will remain a British subject ordinarily ... United Kingdom until fulfilment of this Agreement.
or (if not a British subject) that the Artist is and will remain ... domiciled in the United Kingdom until fulfilment of this Agreement.

(b) The Artist is/is not a minor.

(c) The Artist is, to the best of the Artist's knowledge and belief, in such a state of health that the Company will be able to effect insurance under normal conditions upon the Artist against loss, howsoever caused, arising from the Artist's inability to perform the services required hereunder and upon the conditions as to medical examination which are provided in Clause 20 of the B.F.P.A. Equity Agreement.

(d) The Artist will not incur any liabilities on behalf of the Company nor pledge the Company's credit.

(e) The Artist shall comply with all the regulations of the Studios or location (especially the "no smoking" regulation) and that the Artist shall provide at the Artist's own expense such sun-glasses or other protection for the Artist's eyes as the Artist feels necessary while working in the Studios or on location.

SECTION 9.

Consents.

The Artist hereby grants all consents which the Company may require under the Dramatic and Musical Performers Protection Act 1925.

SECTION 10.

Artist's Agent.

Delete if not applicable

The Artist hereby authorises and empowers his Agents **Noel Gay Artists** of **24, Denmark Street, London, W.C.2.** to collect and receive all sums of money payable to the Artist under the terms of this Agreement and declares that the receipt of the said Agents shall be a good and valid discharge of all persons paying such monies to them. The Artist also authorises and empowers the Company to treat with the said Agents on the Artist's behalf on all matters arising out of this engagement.

SECTION 11.

Notices.

All notices to be served by either party hereunder or under the B.F.P.A. Equity Agreement shall be given in writing and sent to the addresses following, that is to say in respect of the Company to **Memorial Enterprises Ltd., 40 Piccadilly, W.1.** and in respect of the Artist to **Noel Gay Artists, 24 Denmark Street, London, W.C.2.**

SECTION 12.

Special Stipulations

Daily Salary. For any days worked by the Artist beyond the Guarantee Period of eight weeks commencing on or about 14th March 1968 he shall receive a Daily Salary of £40 (forty pounds) with a maximum of £80 (eighty pounds) in any one week.

The Guaranteed Sum of £640 (six hundred and forty pounds) covers the Artist's services for one day of post-synching.

The Company shall accord the Artist as good/a credit as any other artist.

AS WITNESS the hands of the parties hereto the day and year first before written

For ....
Memorial Enterprises Ltd. *(The Company)*

....

....
(The Artist)

To be signed by the parent or guardian of a minor :—

I .... *of* ....

....

hereby warrant that I am the legal guardian of the above-named Artist and having read the above Agreement I am satisfied it is for the benefit of the Artist and it is entered into with my full consent and approval.

....
(Guardian)

The South London Press Ltd. (T.U. all Depts.), Elephant & Castle, S.E.1. and Streatham, S.W.16. S.L.P. 2691/6/67.

Deception

Shooting began in March 1968, with Cheltenham College as our first location. For the first few days I was returned to Worcester each evening to play Cliff in John Osborne's *Look Back in Anger*. A car would drive me to and from Cheltenham. I was encouraged to wear my school uniform as much as possible to break it in. I also had a room in a guest house in Cheltenham, along with Malcolm and Richard. Lindsay had said that he didn't want the three of us to mix socially with the actors playing the Prefects – Robert Swann, Peter Sproule, Michael Cadman and Hugh Thomas – because he wanted there to be a distance, an aloofness between us. For this reason the Prefects were lodged in a guest house a few streets away. Needless to say, Malcolm, Richard and I took no notice of Lindsay's wishes, and set off to visit them very soon after we all arrived. We all went out for a drink and got on extremely well. But we didn't tell Lindsay. In fact, Malcolm and I were both older than all of the 'Prefects'. Hugh Thomas, playing the Himmler-like Denson, was only eighteen, on his way up to Oxford University, from where I had graduated two years earlier.

During the first days of shooting, Malcolm, Richard and I were working quite hard, but never in one of our important scenes. We were used almost as extras. For example, in the Combined Cadet Force marching scene, in which the school, dressed in army uniform, march off on parade, accompanied by brass band music, the three of us are all there, marching away, but the camera doesn't single us out. Similarly, in the first chapel scene, we are simply sitting amongst all the other boys, most of them extras who were attending Cheltenham College for real. The reason, Lindsay said, was that he wanted us to get to know each other, and to be comfortable with the whole filming process before embarking on our dialogue scenes. Filming at Cheltenham continued for several days and included scenes in the town as well as at the school. The very first scene to be shot was a rugby sequence, in which the new assistant master, played by Ben Aris, is tackled to the ground by the juniors. Richard was in the scene, acting as linesman, but Malcolm and I were not required. However, we obviously wanted to go along and watch. As we all sat in the catering tent, awaiting the big moment, Lindsay stood and shouted, in an American accent, 'Let's go make pictures!'

Lindsay had been a pupil at Cheltenham College. Apparently it wasn't the first school invited to hire out their facilities for *If....*, but Lindsay, being an old boy, managed to persuade the headmaster of Cheltenham, David Ashcroft, to allow him to film there for three weeks during term time. Filming in the chapel, the quadrangle and in the grounds and in classrooms had to be fitted around the school's timetable, but having lots of real boys as extras was a bonus. I remember thinking that Mr Ashcroft had taken a somewhat brave decision to allow filming, bearing in mind that the surface content of the film was very critical of public school traditions. It was not until my first day in Cheltenham that I discovered a possible reason for Mr Ashcroft's approval.

Settling into my room at the guest house, I had a visitor. It was Neville Thompson, the assistant to the producers. He welcomed me, then said he had brought me the script. I replied that I already had one, and had been learning my dialogue. 'No, no,' said Neville. And he thrust into my hand a volume considerably slimmer than the actual script. This turned out to be the dummy script. We were to carry this whenever inside Cheltenham College. We were never to take the real script with us to the location. I suppose the theory was, that if the dummy script was left lying around, or even lost, there would be little in it to reveal much of the real action and dialogue of the film.

There are several innocent scenes, not in the real script, including a history class that cycles to a Norman castle, where the teacher lectures disinterested boys about an old feudal story of Celtic loyalty versus the Royal cause. Interestingly, the shooting of the Chaplain is included, although it reads as a surreal fantasy moment. The vicious beating scene, in which the Prefects, led by Rowntree, the head boy, inflict punishment on the three of us, is deftly skated over. Rowntree calls in Wallace, Travis and Knightly (my character's surname) and tells them that they are wasting the most important years of their school lives, behaving like idiots. '*He issues some kind of general punishment and perhaps orders them to go on Barnes's afternoon runs for a week.*' Whether or not Mr Ashcroft would have allowed us to film at Cheltenham, had he seen the actual script, who can say?

The dummy script

20

55. Contd.

HYMN
Love so amazing, so divine,
Demands my heart, my life, my all...
Amen.

The BOYS surge forward to take their buns and milk from the top table.

ROWNTREE presses the bell on the top table and announces that as soon as they have finished they are to go to their rooms and wait.

PEANUTS gestures at JOHNNY as if to say "Who is it?"

JOHNNY shrugs.

56. INT. JUNIOR COMMON ROOM. NIGHT

The JUNIOR BOYS in the Common Room sit at their desks.

BRUNNING mouths across at PHILIPS - "Who is it?"

57. INT. STUDY CORRIDOR. NIGHT

The older BOYS sitting in their studies. Their doors are open. The corridor is empty.

DENSON
(voice over)
Travis! Wallace! Knightly!

The three boys - MICK, JOHNNY and WALLACE - emerge from their studies and walk together down the corridor.

58. INT. PREFECTS' ROOM. NIGHT

A knock on the door.

ROWNTREE calls in WALLACE, TRAVIS and KNIGHTLY and addresses them.

He tells them that he knows that they are wasting the most important years of their school life in mobbing around. They are supposed to be intelligent people and could get to university but instead are behaving like idiots. They may think that they are being very clever but they are behaving like children and should grow up or they will become the laughing stock of the whole House.

He issues some kind of general punishment and perhaps orders them to go on Barnes's afternoon runs for a week.

A page of the dummy script

3

Shooting

Lindsay encouraged us to see rushes, which was sometimes a bit daunting. Seeing yourself on screen is not really the most pleasant experience! But I suppose it can be instructive. In Cheltenham, rushes were screened at the local Odeon, late in the evening when the cinema had closed to the public. On one occasion the creative team sat in the Stalls. We actors were up in the Circle. But we could hear the conversations below. Lindsay and Miroslav Ondricek, the brilliant Czech cinematographer, discussed each sequence through the interpreter, Jirina. We watched several takes of the first chapel scenes, in which boys and staff sing a hymn, followed by a lesson read by Rowntree. Each take had been filmed in colour and in black and white. It became apparent that Lindsay and Mirek (as everyone called Miroslav) felt that colour made the chapel scene less real. The big stained glass window looked almost gaudy and theatrical. We heard Lindsay make the decision to print the black and white takes, which had more of a documentary feel.

Later, Lindsay wrote that there was also a problem for Mirek in that he could not guarantee consistency of colour for the chapel scenes without the use of more lamps, which the budget wouldn't allow. So the chapel scenes are in black and white as are several other scenes in the film. But these are all for artistic reasons rather than financial ones. Some commentators have suggested that we ran out of colour film near the end of shooting, but that is nonsense. Many of the black and white scenes were in fact shot very early on in the schedule. And there is no logical division of fantasy and reality to be found in an analysis of the colour scenes and the black and white scenes. I believe that if it looked better in black and white, black and white was chosen.

One of the assistant directors was Stephen Frears, later to become a much-respected film director in his own right. Stephen didn't endear himself to us actors, because he insisted we took part in his regular morning roll call and uniform inspection, for which all of us, actors and extras alike, had to stand in line while Stephen, like a Sergeant Major, walked along commenting! I have to admit that sometimes Malcolm, Richard and I managed to avoid this ritual, feeling that we were behaving, like our characters, in a rebellious way.

Another assistant director, called Tim, kept me company during my nerve wracking day on Cheltenham College chapel roof. The final sequences in the film, which involved Malcolm, Richard and me, plus Christine Noonan as The Girl, firing down at the parents and dignitaries emerging from Speech Day, were filmed long before most of the interior scenes in the dormitories, school hall and studies. It seemed rather odd to be filming the climax so early. To reach the roof of the chapel involved climbing a series of rickety ladders. I seem to remember chickening out of this, and being carried up from the quadrangle on the work platform of what we called a cherry picker. But I took one look at the sloping roof and the castellated low wall and predicted to Tim that Lindsay would want me to run up one side of the roof, appearing in camera shot as I came to the top, then run down the slope with my sten gun, fling myself against the parapet and fire several shots. I was correct.

Lindsay came up on the cherry picker and directed me to do just that. There was no rehearsal of the action or of the firing of the sten gun. The whole thing felt way out of my comfort zone. I was never a particularly athletic person. I don't like heights very much. And I had never before held a gun, let alone fired one.

We had a delightful ex-military gentleman advising us. He showed me how to hold the sten gun and how to pull the trigger. I remember he showed me a hole somewhere near where my left hand would be. 'Don't put your finger in there,' he warned me, 'or you might lose it!' I asked if a piece of sellotape might be stuck across the hole to prevent my finger from misbehaving and straying within forbidden territory, but this request was denied.

It took a couple of hours before they got to my shot, during which the occasional cup of tea was sent up by cherry picker. Tim and I sat talking, putting the world to rights. When my big moment came, it all seemed to go rather well. Up the slope of the roof, down the other side. Lean against the parapet. Fire sten gun. At this point I felt an excruciating pain in my right ear. For some stupid reason I hadn't thought about the noise. Nor had anyone else. It had been extremely loud. The ringing in my ear continued for several days, then decreased gradually to the constant, but liveable with, whine I hear to this day. Cotton wool was immediately brought, but too late, of course! The final couple of takes weren't as painful, but the ringing continued. Many years later, an ear specialist told me that the top register of high notes had been wiped out in my right ear. This explains why if I sleep on my left side I cannot hear the alarm clock.

Malcolm and I enjoyed filming the scenes in Cheltenham High Street and on a nearby roundabout. The idea was that Mick and Johnny had escaped from school where they should have been supporting the rugby team, then, handcuffed to each other, play out a kind of breaking-free scene from the movies. Our wrists were clamped together in handcuffs as we ran across a busy road, over the grassed roundabout, then over the road again. A sports car screeched to a halt, missing us by a few inches (I never quite knew whether that was planned or not) and at one point I stumbled, and Malcolm had to help me up. This had not been planned, and may have upset the timing, but we lived to tell the tale. This sequence was strangely prophetic, in that a couple of years later, Malcolm was similarly handcuffed to Robert Shaw in Joseph Losey's film *Figures in a Landscape.*

On Cheltenham High Street, Malcolm and I, no longer handcuffed together, had to perform a mock-fight. Malcolm pretends to threaten me with a razor. He slashes. Then we fight and end up rolling on the ground. The camera was on the other side of the road, which meant that occasionally large vehicles would obscure the action, or the traffic would stop, ruining the shot. Large crowds had gathered on the pavement behind the camera. I was unsure whether the passers-by on our side were extras or not. They seemed to be genuine Cheltenham folk, most of whom showed absolutely no interest or concern in our behaviour. However, during one take, an elderly lady stopped and looked challengingly at Malcolm, who stared back at her. She came to look at me, lying prone, then looked at Malcolm again and walked away. It's a lovely humorous moment in the film, but I still don't know whether she was 'real' or not. What was definitely real was the screech of brakes that interrupted the scene where at one point, I was lying on the pavement and Malcolm was apparently beating me up. Suddenly a huge lorry stopped, and an even larger lorry driver jumped down from his cab wielding a hammer. He shouted furious abuse at Malcolm in a most public-spirited way, angrily ticking him off for attacking me. Malcolm, displaying his usual bravado, didn't immediately stop acting and try to explain to the lorry driver that we were making a film. He carried on in character and started defending his actions, saying that I had started the fight and deserved everything I got! Thankfully, before the man could effectively employ his hammer, someone from the film crew dashed over and explained the situation. Somewhat sheepishly, he climbed back into his cab and drove off to wild cheering from the onlookers.

if... 4

Direction

At first, Lindsay surprised me as a director, because he rarely seemed to 'direct' the actors. Yes, he staged the scene, but very often let it evolve organically, before deciding to go for a take. But he rarely seemed to offer advice about character or how to say a line. These were things that I had found most directors concentrated on in the theatre. All became clear after a few days, when Lindsay approached me looking rather serious. 'What's the matter with you?' he asked. 'Wandering around with a worried look on your face. What's the matter?' I balefully bleated that I was never sure that I was doing what he wanted. I pointed out that at the end of a scene, once the gate was checked for unwanted hairs, he would simply shout, 'On!' and walk away. I suppose I was wanting him to bolster my ego at the end of each scene by saying 'Well done' or 'Thank you, that was good'. But that wasn't his way. Lindsay stared at me, somewhat angrily, and simply but forcefully said, 'I took six months to cast this film!' He walked away. Thinking about it, I realised this was the greatest boost of confidence Lindsay could have given me. He was really saying, 'How dare you question my judgement? I cast you because I wanted you here, so I don't have to keep on praising your performance'. From then on, I relaxed and began to enjoy the whole process.

That didn't mean, of course, that Lindsay never made suggestions or even corrections to a performance. But he had a very clever, almost epigrammatic way of explaining things. For example, in the scene in which we clear stuff from under the stage, I had not realised, as we rehearsed the scene, that we were doing it as a punishment from the headmaster. This meant that when I emerged from a trapdoor wearing a gasmask and carrying a stuffed alligator, I was unsure of my motivation! I popped my head out, looked both ways, then climbed up carefully. Lindsay stopped me. 'What are you doing that for?' he asked. I replied that I was looking to see if anybody was coming, because perhaps we shouldn't be doing this. Lindsay shook his head, smiled and came out with a phrase I have never forgotten. He said, 'The more exotic the idea, the more matter of fact we play it.' For the next rehearsal I just lifted out the alligator with Richard as though it was something I did every day of my life. This, I think, helped the somewhat surreal nature of the scene to work. We shot it in one take.

Lindsay had a very appealing and reassuring self-confidence. Some might have perceived it as arrogance. I remember on set one day he told us in a loud voice, addressing cast and crew, that his films would never date, 'apart from the odd skirt length'. He said he would prove it to us by arranging for a late-night showing of *This Sporting Life* at the Odeon, Cheltenham. Seeing this earlier film of his, I think we could understand what he meant.

He was interested in people's feelings and relationships, irrespective of the setting or time. Looking at *If....* nearly fifty years after it was made, I don't think anyone imagines they are watching a 'period' film. This is helped, of course, by the traditional nature of our school uniforms, the kind still worn by Eton schoolboys today. Also, Mick's idealism and desire for freedom can be seen as universal.

Clearing the stuffed alligator from under the stage, with Rupert Webster (Bobby Phillips) and Richard Warwick (Wallace)

While we were in Cheltenham, Peter Brayham, our gentle giant of a stunt coordinator, gave me some lessons in fencing, in preparation for the energetic and flamboyant duelling scene in the gym. I had never fenced before, and began to wish that I had been to a drama school, where basic fencing moves are often taught. Malcolm and Richard were both rather good, and I still cringe when watching the scene, as I move in a stilted fashion, jabbing with my weapon and curling up my other hand in a very strange position. Peter was also giving the occasional lesson to Malcolm in motorbike riding. They used, to begin with, a machine that could be described as a pop-pop, with very little power. Malcolm, as always, displayed no nerves in learning to ride the machine, and didn't seem too concerned that the one he would be riding in the film was a mighty 800 plus cc model. I began to feel nervous, knowing that I would be riding pillion, and that I would have no control whatsoever over our progress. Furthermore, when we came to film the notorious café scene, I found that we were not going to be wearing safety helmets, and that I would be wearing a long, red Isadora Duncan-style scarf! The first session on the bike didn't go too badly. We only had to approach the café at moderate speed, stop, park and walk in. All went fine. There was not much traffic on the road and Malcolm controlled the powerful bike well, even though I don't think he had a licence or had ever taken a test.

We had arrived early at the Packhorse café, which was a real transport café. I have read since that it was on the A5 near Dunstable, but I cannot be sure. Each day we were ferried to a location without us taking much interest in where we filmed. The café had been hired for the day. Not wanting to lose business, the proprietors opened a side window from the kitchen, in order to serve the regular lorry driver customers their breakfast. Meanwhile, inside the café, Lindsay took us through the basic blocking of the scene. Malcolm and I arrive and walk to the counter, where we suddenly see The Girl. We order coffee. Malcolm tries to kiss The Girl, who hits him hard. This leads into Malcolm selecting a disc at

In the café with Christine Noonan (The Girl)
and Malcolm McDowell (Mick)
© Paramount

the jukebox. The music instigates a stylised tiger fight between him and The Girl. Christine Noonan, the beautiful young actress for the role of The Girl, had amazing eyes. She was feisty, too. When told by Lindsay to hit Malcolm really hard, she did just that. It took him by surprise and looked great on camera. The tiger fight involved them rolling around on the floor. Meanwhile, I was sitting quietly at a table with my coffee. At the end of the rehearsal, Lindsay told us to relax while Mirek and the electricians lit the scene, ready to shoot. As Malcolm and Christine dusted themselves off, they approached the table where I was sitting, to join me for a 'real' cup of coffee and a rest. Malcolm said jokingly, referring to the rolling around on the floor, 'Lindsay'll have us doing it naked next!' We all laughed, but were suddenly aware that Lindsay, overhearing nearby, had gone very quiet. 'Malcolm,' he said, 'I think you might have just had the most wonderful idea.'

As I remember it, this is how the notorious nude scene was conceived. It certainly wasn't in the script. The stage direction for the climax of the scene only says, 'they are on the ground – she is on top of him. MICK puts up his hand to shield his face – THE GIRL buries her teeth in his hand.'

Lindsay asked Malcolm and Christine if they would be willing to do a nude scene. He promised to empty the set of all but essential crew. He gave them time to think about it and wandered away. Malcolm seemed to be kicking himself for having, even in jest, suggested the idea, but wasn't unwilling to do it. Christine turned to me and asked my opinion. This came as a surprise. We had only met for the first time that morning. But Malcolm and I were the only two actors there, and, in the circumstances, I was the only peer she could consult. She was a year younger than me. We were both married. I asked if this might make a difference. What would be the reaction of her husband? Christine replied that she wasn't worried about that at all. I suggested she rang her agent for advice. But Christine didn't have an agent. This was only her second job, following an engagement at Ipswich Rep, playing Gigi. My personal opinion was as undecided as hers. I could see that such a scene, in the 1960s, would be regarded as controversial and even scandalous. It would attract publicity. But of the right kind? And might it have a damaging effect on her career?

Eventually Christine agreed and the scene was filmed. It is in black and white, like the rest of the café scene. Some people identify this moment as when the fantasy starts, though there are other black and white sequences earlier in the film. For me, the tiger sequence, including the nudity, suggests a kind of teenage wishful thinking. At the end of the wrestling sequence, the action snaps straight back to the three of us at the café table. This suggests to me that Mick's exciting adventure with The Girl is in his head. Whether or not Lindsay had already intended Malcolm and Christine to suddenly be naked in the scene, who knows? If so, he stage managed it very cleverly, and Malcolm's remark paved the way. As I remember it, however, it was not something that was planned.

Not long after *If....* came out, I was interviewed for a major film role by an American producer. He first flattered me by saying how much he had enjoyed my performance, but then started peppering me with prurient questions about the nude scene. Was I involved? Was I on the set when it was filmed? I replied that indeed I was not. Lindsay had kept his word to Christine. The set was closed to all except him, Mirek and the camera operator. I wondered later if the producer's disappointment with my answers was the reason I wasn't offered a role in his film.

Sitting watching Mick and The Girl embark on their 'fight', my character Johnny smiles and thoughtfully puts Mick's saucer on top of his cup of coffee, in order to keep it warm until his return. This tiny moment has often been mentioned with affection by people seeing the film. This always pleases me, because it was my idea! Lindsay wanted a shot of me looking with a quizzical smile towards the jukebox, Mick and The Girl. I felt I wanted to do something, and the somewhat domestic thought of keeping Mick's coffee hot for him entered my head. I suppose I thought that it was possible Mick could be away some time.

The choice of music coming from the jukebox is particularly haunting and effective. I believe that the choice of the Sanctus from the African *Missa Luba* was Malcolm's. It worked a treat, building to a euphoric climax, echoing or encouraging the abandonment of Mick and The Girl.

5

Privilege

One of the bonuses for me of working on *If....* was meeting and sometimes sharing scenes with some of my favourite older character actors. A year or so earlier I had seen Mona Washbourne playing a monstrous mother in Bill MacIlwraith's play *The Anniversary*. She gave a wonderful performance. Now here she was playing the Matron, licking her lips sensuously as she ladled out platefuls of unappetising stew, or shining a torch at junior boys' genitals.

Graham Crowden had made me sick with laughter playing Colonel Melkett in Peter Shaffer's play *Black Comedy*. Now Graham's inimitable eccentricity and comedy timing was on full display as I sat behind my school desk. He played the history master, who rode a bicycle into the classroom. It was hard to keep a straight face.

As an extra at Chichester Festival Theatre in 1963, I had worked alongside Anthony Nicholls, but never spoken to him. Now I got the chance. In *If....* he played General Denson, giving the traditional Speech Day address, determined to keep going even when smoke is pouring from under the stage. And, of course, there was Arthur Lowe. It was a rare treat to watch him nervously welcome us boys back for the start of the new term. As a weak housemaster, he clearly had no influence in the running of the school. The Prefects conducted their own cruel regime.

When we shot the welcome scene in the panelled school hall, Malcolm, Richard and I were sitting at one of the tables at right angles to the platform, where the teachers gathered. We were quite near the front. Arthur's wary welcome speech was so funny it made us corpse. Lindsay became so incensed with our behaviour that we were sent out of the dining hall with no close-ups! Looking back, it would be easy to think that my admiration and affection for Arthur Lowe was the result of his brilliant Captain Mainwaring in *Dad's Army*. But this would be untrue. The first episode of *Dad's Army* wasn't screened until later in 1968, the year we filmed *If....* But he was definitely an actor I recognised and respected, possibly from his television appearances as Mr Swindley in *Coronation Street*. Like Mona, Graham and Anthony, Arthur was a 'regular' in Lindsay's repertory company of reliable older character actors. Others were Ralph Richardson, Dandy Nichols and Leonard Rossiter. All had a quirky, eccentric quality on screen. I think Lindsay enjoyed their ability to play comedy with total truth.

6

Discipline

The welcome scene was filmed not at Cheltenham, but at Aldenham School, near Watford. It was generally agreed that Aldenham was a pretty ghastly establishment in all sorts of ways. Apparently the dormitory in which we filmed had looked so drab and spartan that Lindsay insisted it should be repainted. Otherwise, he said nobody would believe it. But, after shooting, the film company had to agree to redecorate it back to its original ugliness.

At Aldenham, as at Cheltenham, we had no dressing rooms as such, and no green room. It was suggested that when we were not working, we 'boys' could relax at one end of the school library, while the other end was reserved for the 'grown-up' actors. On one occasion, Arthur Lowe was sitting alone at that end of the library, reading a book, while at our end, several of us were chatting, in rather inconsiderately loud voices. We discussed Aldenham School, agreeing that it appeared to be a terrible place, and that any parent who sent their child there had to be an idiot or a sadistic monster. Throughout our tirade, Arthur scarcely moved a muscle. It was not until many years later that I discovered his son Stephen had been a pupil there at that very time.

Spartan Aldenham also surprised us with the only outdoor showers I have ever seen, except by a sunny swimming pool! It was a chilly day in April when we shot the shower sequence, in which the Prefect Denson gives the three of us cold punishment showers. The day mainly involved being showered with cold water, then, between takes, drying our hair in the warmth of an industrial blower heater, before getting back under the shower. I think Richard and I were treated kindly, in that the water was only cold enough to avoid any steam being visible. We didn't suffer as much as Malcolm. By now his bravado was well known, so the crew mischievously made sure that his shower was icy cold. This was arguably a good thing, in that Malcolm's reactions look, and probably are, extremely realistic.

While each of us took our punishment, the others stood waiting, our modesty sometimes protected by a towel, sometimes not. The necessity to shoot the scene in several different ways, to make sure every possible censor would be satisfied, meant that we did every sequence over and over again. It wasn't our most enjoyable day.

Another Aldenham scene that was, for the time, potentially risqué or controversial was the night time scene in the dormitory, panning across sleeping faces, finally settling on Richard as Wallace and young Bobby Phillips sleeping together. In the film I think it comes across as something of beauty rather than repugnance. Indeed the earlier scene in which Bobby Phillips watches admiringly as Wallace performs acrobatics has the same tender, poetic quality. On the day the dormitory scene was shot, I remember there was a flutter of activity among the various assistant directors, because it was rumoured that the mother of Rupert Webster (Bobby Phillips) was visiting the set that day. Plans were put in force to divert her from the dormitory until the bed scene had been completed. In fact, Rupert's mother was the much-respected actress, Heather Chasen. It is unlikely that she would have been shocked.

The brutality of the beating scene in the gym is what spurs Mick, Knightly and Wallace to stage their revolt. The scene may not be included in the dummy script, but in the actual script, it is

In the dormitory

very fully described. Lindsay had decided that the audience would not see Wallace and Knightly's punishment in the gym. The camera would stay in the adjoining changing room, watching us prepare for our ordeal, then return to be met by a sympathetic Mick. Then, in a dramatic development, Lindsay cuts to inside the gym as Mick enters, and the camera stays there to witness him being beaten. This offered the chance for a build-up of tension, particularly bearing in mind that Mick receives twice the number of strokes of the cane as the other two. The decision was also made to film the build-up in the changing room in one long take. In a way it became an improvisation, but Lindsay was very careful to ensure the timing was correct.

He assembled the Prefects in the gym. None of them would be seen in the shot. He instructed Robert Swann (Rowntree) to issue all the relevant instructions to Richard and me: to take off our coats, to bend over the wall bars, receive four strokes, then stand, walk to Rowntree, shake his hand and say 'thank you'. This would be repeated with Mick once the scene transferred to the gym. Robert as Rowntree ran up from the end of the gym to the wall bars and brought the cane down hard on a mat or cushion, to provide the right sound. Richard and I were grateful not to be asked to actually undergo the punishment!

Once the structure of the scene had been established, we simply ran it. We knew that Wallace received only four strokes, and that Mick and Knightly, listening from the changing room, would appear relieved that the punishment wasn't worse. We also knew from the script that when Wallace returned, he would lower his trousers to reveal the fact that blood had been drawn. The one improvised addition to the script occurred when I was in the gym, receiving my four strokes. Malcolm looked through the gap in the double doors and suddenly reacted with the line, 'Christ, that was a bit low!' I think we all enjoyed shooting this scene, in which the off-stage action was dictating our reactions. Later, of course, Malcolm had to endure the real punishment. Although he had some paper – exercise books, I seem to remember – stuffed down his trousers,

70

MICK

Yes ... I have.
(slowly)
... The thing I hate about you, Rowntree, is this way you give Coca Cola to your Scum and your best teddy bear to Oxfam ... and expect us to lick your frigid fingers for the rest of your frigid life.

ROWNTREE ruffled, cracks the foil against the table.

ROWNTREE

Go down to the gymnasium. Wait outside.

81 INT. HOUSE CORRIDORS NIGHT

Feet echoing on the planks.

MICK, JOHNNY and WALLACE walk quickly down the corridor between the partitions ... behind which the rest of the HOUSE waits listening.

They arrive outside the gym doors and stand waiting.

The noise of the WHIPS' feet, marching in unison.

The FOUR WHIPS march straight past MICK, JOHNNY and WALLACE and go straight into the gym.

JOHNNY, pressed flat against the wall.
Wets his lips.

MICK smiles across at him and at WALLACE.

DENSON
(voice over)

Wallace.

WALLACE knocks on the gym door and enters.

JOHNNY and MICK listen.
They hear the strokes.

Their mouths move silently as they count.

When it stops at four they look at each other as if it to say 'not so bad.'

The door opens.

Two pages of my official script

71

WALLACE appears.

WALLACE

Only four.

JOHNNY knocks and enters the gym.

WALLACE performs a couple of boxing feints, then suddenly unbelts his trousers and takes them down. MICK inspects his bottom.

WALLACE

Blood?

MICK

Blood.

From inside the gym comes the sound of the foil hitting JOHNNY - like rifle shots.

JOHNNY appears at the gym door.

MICK knocks.

82 INT. GYMNASIUM NIGHT

The FOUR WHIPS stand in front of the huge wooden horse.

MICK moves through the black hanging ropes and waits in front of the FOUR WHIPS.

ROWNTREE

Take your coat off. Go to the bars. Head under the bars - hands on top.

MICK bends double with the back of his head against the bars, holding on like a monkey to the bars above.

ROWNTREE - on the other side of the gym - raises the blade high above his head, and charges MICK.

MICK takes the blow.

ROWNTREE walks back for another run.

MICK is a motionless, doubled-up figure at the end of the gym.

nevertheless the impact of each stroke of the cane was considerable. And Robert as Rowntree was encouraged not to cheat the athletic run-up and solid swish of the cane.

The sequence in which General Denson arrives to make the speech on Founders' Day, leading into the mass evacuation from the hall, necessitated by us Crusaders lighting a fire under the stage, followed by the massacre in the quadrangle was, of course, a major set piece of the film. The three of us, plus Christine as The Girl and Rupert Webster as Bobby Phillips, only featured in this sequence in our positions on the roof of the school and the Cheltenham College chapel, firing down on the parents, staff, prefects and other boys below. Most of our shots didn't involve those on the ground. They were shot separately. This meant that we were not called on the days when a troupe of extras – many of them dressed up as though they were going to a wedding – arrived, along with elderly gentlemen dressed in suits of armour, and a very impressive-looking Bishop. Most of these extras had been recruited locally and were full of enthusiasm. I decided, along with the others, not to miss the fun and, although we were not allowed into St John's Church that doubled as the school hall (it has since been demolished), we were able to witness the exciting scenes in the quadrangle, complete with explosives tossing large chunks of turf into the air, 'parents' scuttling to safety and gamely pretending to be shot and playing dead or injured. Encouraged by Lindsay, they entered into the spirit of the filming with immense gusto. We were very impressed by the upper-class sounding lady who grabbed a sten gun and aimed it up at us (sadly we weren't up on the roof at the time!) shouting, 'Bastards, bastards!' It wasn't until much later that we discovered she was the mother of Lindsay's Royal Court Theatre associate, Anthony Page.

7

Prophesy

It was fun to occasionally go on location somewhere other than a school. The surreal scene in which the Headmaster tells us off for shooting the Chaplain, who then appears to be resurrected by rising out of a drawer, was filmed in a building in Knightsbridge. Peter Jeffrey, playing the Headmaster, showed immense self-control as he admonished us, then pulled open the drawer. The three of us were not as well behaved. We kept corpsing, ruining several takes. But seeing Geoffrey Chater as the Chaplain rising with dignity, almost elegance, from inside a chest of drawers was very amusing. This is the scene that Lindsay later admitted might have been a fantasy leap too far. Indeed Harold Pinter apparently told him just that.

For us, this shooting day was made even more enjoyable because we were allowed to go out at lunchtime. Interestingly, playing schoolboys yearning for freedom meant that in real life, we tended to behave like our characters, or at least have fun in each other's company. Wearing our school uniforms we walked to Harrods and went up to the top floor, where the *Way In* department sold wacky clothes. We had a lovely time searching

Looking through the window of the motorcycle showroom, smoking a cigarette
© Paramount

through the rails and commenting on the suits and shirts, while the staff became concerned that we were up to no good.

The scene in the motor cycle showroom was shot in Wimbledon. It was a real showroom in Gladstone Road, which disappeared some years ago to become a Wetherspoon's pub. By coincidence, four decades later, my daughter and her husband lived for a while just a few doors away. My mother and stepfather came to see what was going on. Their car, a blue Morris Minor, registration number 8000 BP can be seen in the back of several shots, particularly when Malcolm and I are looking in the showroom window. It doesn't say in the script that we should be smoking, but Malcolm and I obviously decided we thought it would be a good idea. Having fled from the school to freedom, smoking a cigarette was symbolic of our improved status. Lindsay must have agreed. I remember I instinctively held my cigarette in the way in which I used to as a young teenager, hiding it from adult view. The lighted end was pointing towards my palm rather than extending through my fingers. This involved sucking the filter in what I thought was a suitably secretive manner. Ellis Dale was splendid as the salesman, looking at us somewhat suspiciously, then suddenly reacting to the sound of the revved up engine as Malcolm set off, whistling to me to jump on the back. Great fun.

We shot the study scenes at Merton Park Studios. Lindsay had purposely scheduled these scenes for the later stages of filming, so that Malcolm, Richard and I could get to know each other and be familiar enough with the filming process to work on these more intimate scenes. The day before shooting started we decorated our studies with the pictures we had been asked to collect from magazines. To these were added others from the design department. Lindsay became involved, too, in positioning certain pictures in more noticeable sites.

Filming these scenes coincided with the beginnings of the Paris student riots. I remember Lindsay waving a newspaper in the air, delighted that *If....* could be seen as prophetic. I think he was a bit annoyed that we hadn't made the film and released it some months

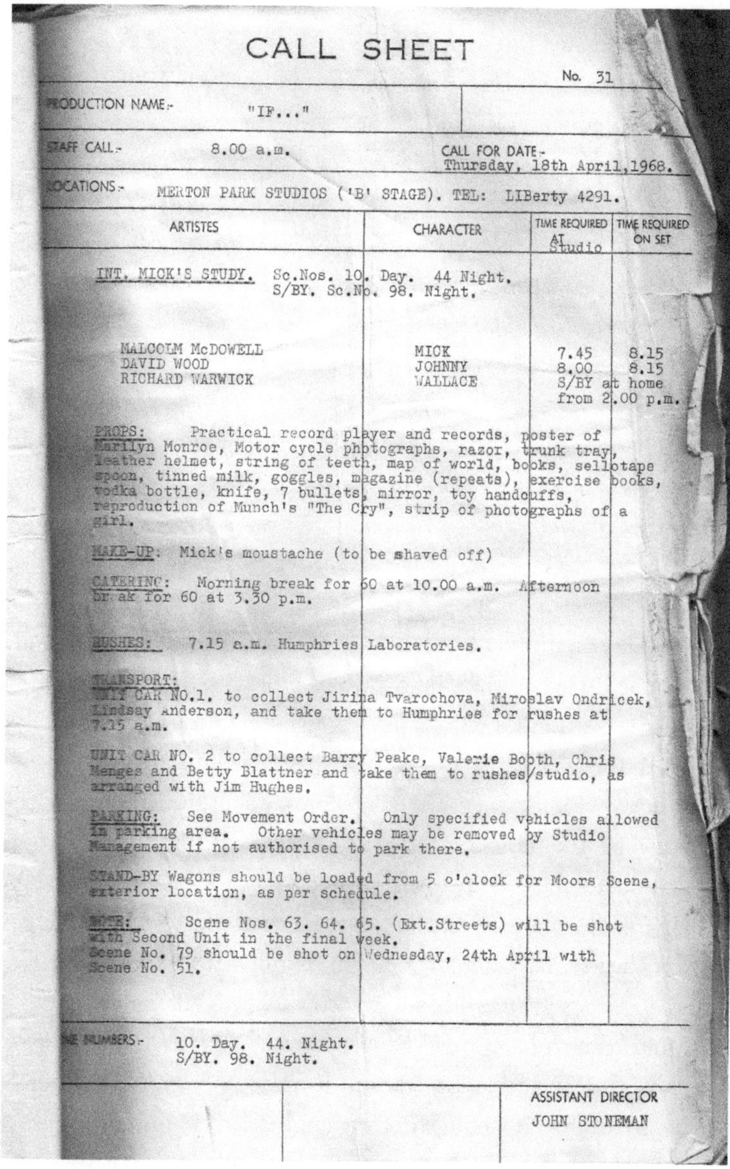

CALL SHEET

No. 31

ODUCTION NAME:- "IF..."	
AFF CALL:- 8.00 a.m.	CALL FOR DATE:- Thursday, 18th April,1968.
OCATIONS:- MERTON PARK STUDIOS ('B' STAGE). TEL: LIBerty 4291.	

ARTISTES	CHARACTER	TIME REQUIRED AT Studio	TIME REQUIRED ON SET
INT. MICK'S STUDY. Sc.Nos. 10. Day. 44 Night. S/BY. Sc.No. 98. Night.			
MALCOLM McDOWELL	MICK	7.45	8.15
DAVID WOOD	JOHNNY	8.00	8.15
RICHARD WARWICK	WALLACE	S/BY at home from 2.00 p.m.	

PROPS: Practical record player and records, poster of Marilyn Monroe, Motor cycle photographs, razor, trunk tray, leather helmet, string of teeth, map of world, books, sellotape spoon, tinned milk, goggles, magazine (repeats), exercise books, vodka bottle, knife, 7 bullets, mirror, toy handcuffs, reproduction of Munch's "The Cry", strip of photographs of a girl.

MAKE-UP: Mick's moustache (to be shaved off)

CATERING: Morning break for 60 at 10.00 a.m. Afternoon break for 60 at 3.30 p.m.

RUSHES: 7.15 a.m. Humphries Laboratories.

TRANSPORT:
UNIT CAR NO.1. to collect Jirina Tvarochova, Miroslav Ondricek, Lindsay Anderson, and take them to Humphries for rushes at 7.15 a.m.

UNIT CAR NO. 2 to collect Barry Peake, Valerie Booth, Chris Menges and Betty Blattner and take them to rushes/studio, as arranged with Jim Hughes.

PARKING: See Movement Order. Only specified vehicles allowed in parking area. Other vehicles may be removed by Studio Management if not authorised to park there.

STAND-BY Wagons should be loaded from 5 o'clock for Moors Scene, exterior location, as per schedule.

NOTE: Scene Nos. 63. 64. 65. (Ext.Streets) will be shot with Second Unit in the final week.
Scene No. 79 should be shot on Wednesday, 24th April with Scene No. 51.

E NUMBERS:- 10. Day. 44. Night.
S/BY. 98. Night.

ASSISTANT DIRECTOR
JOHN STONEMAN

A call sheet

earlier, so that it could have been in cinemas before the Paris riots hit the headlines. I certainly don't think he wanted the world to think the riots had inspired his film.

In an article in *The Times* on November 29th 1968, a week before the première, Elizabeth Sussex wrote:

Before student violence had begun to hit the headlines, a film was being made which strangely presaged events to come. Lindsay Anderson's If...., made by the production company set up by Albert Finney and Michael Medwin, shows life in what Anderson describes as 'the archetypal English public school'. If.... ends with a violent schoolboy revolution.

'When we were filming,' Anderson told me, 'the photographs in the newspapers suddenly began to look like the stills from If.... It certainly suggests that, when we were working on the script about two years ago, David Sherwin and I were being, to some extent, prophetic. 'To prophesy,' he added, 'seems to me one of the functions of the artist – perhaps the most important function'.

Working on the two-hander and three-hander study scenes within the confined space of the studio gave us more insight into Lindsay's directing process. Although he never suggested inflections and rarely discussed the characters much, he encouraged us to experiment occasionally with the lines. The day before we shot the scene in which we discussed 'the most horrible way to die', Malcolm, Richard and I talked about the scene, failing to understand how different ways of dying could make us end up laughing hysterically. I had a line: 'Cancer's worse. My mother took six months ...' I knew I had to play that seriously. But within seconds, Mick was talking about how he would hate to have a nail banged through the back of his neck – slowly. This, in the script, leads to hysteria, in which we all join. Unable to see how it would work, we approached Lindsay. He didn't argue with our criticism of the scene. He simply said that we were quite right, it was a terrible bit of writing, and the best thing would be for us to come in an hour early the next day, improvise around the scene, and find a better way to do it. Gratefully we left.

Next morning, on the set, but without any technicians present, we started to improvise the scene. It began to sort of make sense. The technicians arrived. We ran the scene and lighting began. Suddenly, Lindsay motioned to Stuart Baird, one of the assistant directors, who shot off, returning moments later with a bottle of whisky. Lindsay invited us all to have a swig. And another swig. Lighting was ready. We were told to stand by. We were given another swig of whisky. The camera turned, Lindsay shouted 'Action' and after a few words, we all dissolved into drunken giggles. 'Pull yourselves together!' roared Lindsay, 'you're meant to be professionals!' We protested in vain that he had given us all whisky at 9am in the morning, so what did he expect? However, after a few takes, the scene was in the can. I certainly remember rolling around with laughter towards the end, and undoubtedly the whisky had loosened us up. The remarkable thing, however, was that it was only when I saw the finished film, months later, that I realised we had played the scene word for word as written in the script. With consummate skill, Lindsay had allowed us to work round the script, under the impression that we were improvising and creating something better, yet by the end of the session he had brought us back to exactly what was on the page. Very impressive.

I don't remember the writer, David Sherwin, being present on this occasion. But he regularly attended the filming, and proved a friendly, if slightly aloof, member of the team. It must have been exciting for him. He was only two years older than Malcolm and me, and this was his first film. It was clear that he and Lindsay had worked together on the script for months, so there appeared to be very few occasions when they discussed a line or suggested a change. I think most of us remembered David particularly for his beautiful assistant – or was she his girlfriend – called Gay, who used to drive him to locations in a rather impressive sports car. We all thought he was very lucky to have such an effervescent sidekick.

The main motor cycle sequence was saved until one of the very last shooting days. It would be cynical to think that the reason for this was that everyone realised there was real danger involved, but it is true to say that if Malcolm and I had been killed, there was still a film in the can. We were to drive fast along a main country road, enter a roundabout, go half way round, then roar off at speed up towards the Packhorse Café, but on the day of shooting I couldn't help overhearing a conversation between Peter Braham, our stunt coordinator, and Michael Medwin, one of our producers. Peter told Michael that he wanted it understood that he could take no responsibility for whatever might happen. You could understand why. Malcolm and I were on a hugely powerful motorbike, travelling on a public road, with no crash helmets and no licence, and probably no insurance! Add to that my Isadora Duncan scarf flying in the breeze, and one could see there was indeed a risk. Lindsay, of course, showed no concern. After the first take he simply encouraged Malcolm to drive faster! I was certainly nervous, if not terrified, mainly because, sitting on the back, I had no control. But in fairness, Malcolm rode the bike well and from time to time yelled over his shoulder, 'All right?' which I found rather reassuring.

We shot more travelling scenes, with the camera alongside us, which seemed to go well. But I was quite relieved when we discussed the shot in which Christine stood on the saddle between us, arms outstretched, personifying freedom, and Lindsay suggested that perhaps it would be safer if someone more accustomed to riding motorbikes stood in for me. So a young local man, face hidden, held on to Christine to help her ride standing upright.

Michael Medwin, our affable producer, often visited the set. He was instantly recognisable to me as one of the stars of the television comedy series, *The Army Game*, which had been hugely popular in the late fifties and early sixties. Michael's rendition of the theme song had even made the hit parade, as we called it then. His partner in the production company, Memorial Enterprises, was Albert Finney, the actor who had come to prominence when he took over the role of Shakespeare's *Coriolanus* from an indisposed Laurence Olivier. His gritty, working-class hero performance in *Saturday Night and*

Sunday Morning in 1960 must have been noticed by Lindsay, because it was directed by his colleague Karel Reisz. And in 1963 he starred in *Tom Jones,* directed by another of Lindsay's Royal Court Theatre associates, Tony Richardson. I remember being excited to attend a talk by Finney during a drama course given by the British Drama League when I was in my mid-teens. As co-producer of *If....*, we didn't see as much of him as Michael, but it was a thrill to meet him. At about this time, Memorial produced Peter Nichols' moving play *A Day in the Life of Joe Egg* in the West End. Albert subsequently played the lead role on Broadway and won a Tony. He also directed and starred in Memorial's film *Charlie Bubbles.*

John Stoneman was *If....*'s no-nonsense First Assistant. Like all good First Assistants, he shouted a lot, maintained strict discipline on the studio floor and tried to make sure that as little time was wasted as possible. He didn't try to endear himself to anybody, but was appreciated for his efficiency. When I had shot my last scene, John came over to me and, in a surprisingly friendly way, thanked me for my cooperation. Apparently I had always arrived on time, had never been 'difficult' or caused the production team problems. I was grateful and said so. I asked John if he thought the film would be a success. He said that he hoped so very much, although it was probably an 'art film', destined for the Academy cinema in Oxford Street. He also said that he believed *If....* would make Malcolm a star. When I asked him why, he replied that Malcolm always behaved in a manner to get attention. He would often ask for a glass of water, just as everyone else was ready to shoot a scene. He would sometimes be late on set.

I found it sad that these 'qualities' were automatically signs of star quality. I was much happier believing that Malcolm would indeed become a star, thanks to his determination and undoubted talent. In the early days of shooting I hadn't quite understood how effective Malcolm was on screen. But seeing the rushes made me immediately aware of his magnetism and magic. He made no secret of the fact that he was determined to become a star. When shooting finished he decided to turn down all offers of work unless they were major roles in big films. He turned down theatre and television work during the months awaiting the release of *If*..... and lived on the dole in a flat in the North End Road, biding his time. His brave determination paid off. Joseph Losey, having seen him in *If*...., offered him *Figures in a Landscape*, opposite Robert Shaw. Eight years later Malcolm and I worked together again, on Jack Gold's First World War film, *Aces High*. It was fun, and it was easily noticeable how excellent a screen actor Malcolm had become.

Several weeks after the end of shooting, Malcolm, Richard and I were asked to come back for one day, to re-shoot our part of the field trip scene, in which we shoot a hole in the tea urn and then Mick shoots the Chaplain. There were one or two key moments that obviously hadn't come out right on the original shoot. At the time, I was in a revival of *Four Degrees Over*, the revue I co-wrote, at the Salisbury Playhouse, so it was agreed that the filming would be done on a Sunday. The location was to be in a wooded area in Surrey, not far from the flat where I was living. However, it would mean a very early start, so it was suggested that I went home after the Saturday evening show in Salisbury. The production company kindly offered to send a car for me. Imagine my surprise – and considerable excitement – when one of the familiar film unit drivers met me at the Stage Door and took me round the corner to Albert Finney's Rolls Royce! Although Albert was co-producer of *If*.... he was currently out of the country so his Rolls was available! Sadly I was unable to impress my fellow Salisbury actors and stage staff. Reclining in the back, complete with fully-stocked bar, I glided smoothly off to suburban North Cheam, without being seen by a single soul.

I think I earned £80 a week for playing Johnny in *If*.... and we were filming for six weeks or more. Compared with the money I earned in rep, it was a small fortune. It enabled me to buy my first proper car – a Triumph Herald Estate. (At university I had paid £30 for a 1934 Austin Seven, which only managed 100 miles or so

1 An off-camera shot of me as Johnny.
2 Lindsay making me look less tidy. Behind, Stephen Frears and Richard Warwick as Wallace.
3 Lindsay demonstrating how to fall when pretending to be shot.
4 Field Day, with Malcolm McDowell (Mick) and Richard Warwick (Wallace).
5 Sitting in Cheltenham College quadrangle with Sheila, my wife, and Robert Swann (Rowntree).
6 On location. Richard Warwick (Wallace), David Wood (Johnny) and Sheila, my wife.
7 Firing my sten gun from Cheltenham College Chapel roof.
8 The three of us in Mick's study.
9 Me in Mick's study.
10 A serious Johnny in the Headmaster's study.
11 A publicity shot of Malcolm, Richard and me, not in school uniform!

before giving up the ghost). I bought the Triumph Herald from a garage in Worcester where I was back in rep. On my first excursion I excitedly drove to the small town of Ombersley where I parked the car facing a wall and went shopping. It was a Saturday lunchtime. When I came back, I found I was unable to find reverse gear. To my embarrassment, I had to ask passers-by to push me backwards, until I could drive forwards. I had to put my foot down to get back to the theatre in time for the matinee performance. Needless to say, I eventually found the reverse gear and enjoyed driving the car, ever thankful to *If....*, for several years.

8

Reaction

If…. premièred in London on December 5th 1968, as part of the London Film Festival. I was unable to attend because I was in Manchester, acting at the university theatre in a show called *Have You Seen Manchester?.* Regional productions rarely employ understudies, so I knew a trip to London was impossible. I would have loved to have joined Malcolm, Richard and Christine, plus Lindsay and many others involved with the film, but contented myself by reading the newspaper reviews, many of which were very complimentary. Penelope Mortimer, in *The Observer* called *If….* 'Anderson's masterwork'. The *Evening Standard* called it 'brilliant …. vastly entertaining' and *The Sun* found it 'wickedly funny'. The *Daily Mail* admired 'an explosive mixture … sharp, cruel and often brilliantly funny…'. 'A hand-grenade of a film,' said the *Evening News.* 'A masterpiece,' declared the *Sunday Express.*

Lindsay had been concerned that his film wouldn't appeal to a wide audience. In *The Observer* he was quoted as saying, *'How quixotic it suddenly seems, how doomed to failure, this attempt to straddle a divided culture, to find an audience that is neither 'Carry On' nor New Statesman, neither ad-mass nor mandarin.'*

Newspaper advert for the first showing

Yet even John Coleman, in the *New Statesman,* complimented Lindsay saying, '*It is quite the best film he has made*'.

Also opening in December 1968 was my second play for children, *The Owl and the Pussycat Went To See…*, based on the verses and stories of Edward Lear, co-written with Sheila Ruskin, at the Swan Theatre, Worcester. It was the beginning of a fruitful period of my life. *If….* led to a respectable television and stage career as an actor, and *Owl* the following year became a hit show in London, encouraging me to make writing and directing plays for children a much bigger part of my life. In an article in *The Times* in March 1998, Daniel Rosenthal was the first journalist to comment on my two contrasting careers. He wrote:

'Exactly 30 years ago, David Wood was to be found on the roof of Cheltenham College chapel armed with a machine gun, awaiting his cue to begin one of the most notorious bursts of violence in British cinema history.

It feels strange to learn that in 1968 the young actor helping Malcolm McDowell to carry out the climactic massacre in If…. had just written a stage adaptation of Hans Andersen's The Tinder Box, *the first of 40 shows that would earn Wood the unofficial title of children's playwright laureate. By the time his bloody rebellion as Johnny in If…. was shocking the middle-aged, his first wholesome play was delighting the under-tens… The influence of the film's late director, Lindsay Anderson, is a happy legacy. 'Lindsay was never prepared to compromise for the sake of commercial gain', he says, 'and neither am I.'*

Lindsay noticed that I was absent from the première. He wrote to me:

Dear David, I was sorry to find you weren't around when finally the picture hit the screen. I hasten to add that I'm delighted you're working, and was even more delighted to spot you in that TV bit about the show, and to catch your ventriloquist number! This referred to a sketch in *Have You Seen Manchester?* in which I played Trevor Peacock's ventriloquial doll. Lindsay goes on to write about the reviews and his hope that the film will get a fair distribution.

I expect you'll have seen some of our notices which have been pretty good: even more important, the business got off to a smashing start – even though that pre-Christmas week is reckoned to be one of the worst in the year – and seems to be keeping up, for the moment anyway. Now it's up to Paramount to exploit the figures and the notices with ABC and get us some sort of a release. Next week I hope I'll hear something of how all that is going.'

The next paragraph shows how important to Lindsay the technical aspects of film-making were. He needed to be in control of all departments and waged a constant battle against complacency.

'I'm sorry not to have written sooner but it was hectic up to the last moment – we had to open even without a really satisfactory print; the labs have been very difficult and unsatisfactory, and of course having to go through all the business of grading and fighting for a good copy without having a cameraman around (Even Chris has taken himself off to Colombo on some documentary mission) has not been easy. However, we at last seem to have the printing under control (I saw the first good copy on Christmas Eve!) and can move on to the next battles ...'

The final paragraph, in which he shows how much he valued the work of the cast, shows Lindsay's warmth and humanity. His kind words about my performance meant a great deal to me, and made me realise how much I had wanted to please him, how much I respected his refusal to compromise, and what an extraordinary experience he had given me.

'I hope it isn't too late for me to say how very grateful I am to you for all your good work and always generous help through some hard days of that back-breaking schedule. I know I can't really complain about the critics – but I do regret that the overall impact of the picture has a bit resulted in some of the collaborators who made it getting less than their due. And particularly the actors. Because it was such a splendid cast: and your own performance and personality is such an essential part, with all the sensitivity, truthfulness and discretion you gave it, of the success of If....

Thank you David – and all best wishes to you both.

Lindsay.'

57 Greencroft Gardens London NW6 December 29th 1968

Dear David -

I was sorry to find you weren't around when finally the picture hit the screen - though I hasten to add that I'm delighted you're working, and was even more delighted to spot you in that TV bit abou t the show, and to catch your ventriloquist number!

I expect you'll have seen some of our notices, which have been pretty good: even more important, the business got off to a smashing start - even though that pre-Christmas week is reckoned to be one of the worst in th e year - and seems to be keeping up, for the moment anyway. Now its up to Paramount to exploit the figures and the notices with ABC and get us some sort of a release. Next week I hope I'll hear something of how all that is going.

I'm sorry not to have written sooner: but it was hectic up to the last moment - we had to open even without a really satisfactory print; the labs have been very difficult and unsatisfactory, and of course having to go through all the business of grading and fighting for a good copy without having a cameraman around (Even Chris hast taken himself off to Colombo on some documentary mission) has not been easy. However, we at last seem to have the printing under control (I saw the first good copy on Christmas Eve!) and can move on to the next battles.. ..

I hope it isn't too late for me to say how very grateful I am to you for all your good work and always generous help through some hard days of that back-breaking schedule. I know I

The letter Lindsay sent me after the release of the film

-2-

can't really complain about the critics - but I do regret that the overall impact of the picture has a bit resulted in some of the collaborators who made it getting less than their due. And particularly the actors. Because it was such a splendid cast: and your own performance and personality is such an essential part, with all the sensitivity, truthfulness and discretion you gave it, of the success of IF....

Thankyou again, David - and all best wishes to you both,

Lindsay

As a thankyou present, Lindsay sent me a copy of Royston Lambert's book, *The Hothouse Society,* an exploration of boarding-school life through the boys' and girls' own writings. It still sits on my bookshelf, and I treasure it.

If.... opened very successfully in France. A friend returned from Paris and told me the film was showing to packed houses in several cinemas in the city. He said that if I were to walk down the Champs Elysée I would be mobbed! This certainly never happened, but the success of the film there, and later in Japan, was very heartening.

One experience, early in 1969, ensured that success would never be allowed to go to my head, and that my feet would always stay firmly on the ground. I was appearing in *Have You Seen Manchester?* and *If....* had opened to considerable acclaim. A trendy teenage magazine asked to interview me and take a photo. But they couldn't come to Manchester. Simultaneously the cast, including me, of a musical revue called *Three To One On,* in which I had toured earlier in the year, was invited to appear on the Simon Dee BBC TV programme, singing a song from the show. The producers had spotted us on the Edinburgh Festival Fringe earlier in the year. The show, which I also co-wrote, was a follow-up to *Four Degrees Over,* the revue that had transferred to the West End the previous year. Our new show featured a song about the Guinness Book of Records. Simon Dee wanted us to sing it on his show, to be recorded on a Sunday night. My agent evolved a plan whereby early on the Sunday morning I was to fly from Manchester to Heathrow, where I would be met by a journalist in a car. I would be interviewed while being driven to the Shepherd's Bush Empire, where the Simon Dee show was being recorded that afternoon. A photo would also be taken.

Feeling very grand and famous, I set off for Manchester Airport, only to find that fog was delaying all flights. Eventually I took off, only to land a short time later in Liverpool. The cabin crew managed to get a message to the BBC to say I would be late, but I had no contact details for the journalist. As we waited on the runway in

Liverpool, a message came from the BBC saying I would probably be too late to appear on the programme. Doggedly I stayed in my seat. We took off and eventually landed at Heathrow. There was no sign of the journalist, who had obviously waited two or three hours and then given up. I realised I had very little money, not even enough to take a taxi into Shepherd's Bush. This meant boarding an airport bus, which took an eternity to reach the terminus in Cromwell Road, from where I hurried to the Shepherd's Bush Empire. As I arrived, the audience from the television recording were emptying out into the street. I had missed out on being in the television show. I had also missed my magazine interview. Yes, my feet remained firmly on the ground.

On July 5th, 1969, the Rolling Stones performed their now-legendary concert in Hyde Park. Richard Warwick and I spent most of that afternoon in a flat very near the park, the home of a mutual acquaintance called Stephen, who worked at the Arts Council. We ventured out to see the Stones, but never got anywhere near! All we could hear from the back of the crowd was the thudding drum beat of Charlie Watts and the occasional screeching guitar. What I most remember from meeting up with Richard on that day was sharing our mutual disappointment about being left out of the celebrations in Cannes where, a couple of months earlier, *If....* had triumphantly won the Palme d'Or, the film festival's highest award. We knew that Malcolm had been invited, and by then we quite understood that he was much more the rising star than we were. We also knew that he was very much Lindsay's protégé. It was quite right that he should have experienced the atmosphere of Cannes and the excitement of winning. Nevertheless, we had very much seen ourselves as a trio when making the film, and when it had been announced that the film was up for the prize, we had hoped we might be invited too. But no.

Perhaps Memorial Enterprises, our producers, were concerned about the cost of taking us all – and Christine, who should surely have been invited too. Or maybe they rightly realised that *If....*

The cover of the book Lindsay gave me at the end of shooting, plus his inscription inside.

To David

with grateful and affectionate
memories of Johnny
and
IF....

from Lindsay

1968

Front cover photograph by Henry Grant. *The Hothouse Society* published by Weidenfeld and Nicolson, now Orion. Reproduced with permission.

was Lindsay and Malcolm's passport to the big time. Lindsay might not have openly craved commercial success, but he certainly hoped for acceptance and respect from the mainstream film world. And Malcolm definitely deserved the acclaim and the subsequent fame that *If....* gave him.

Lindsay sent me a picture postcard from Cannes. *'Love from Cannes:'* he wrote. *'Showbiz and sunshine – what a disgusting mixture! But then I'm not unbiased....'*

It amused me that he implied he hated the razzmatazz. I suspect he secretly rather enjoyed it.

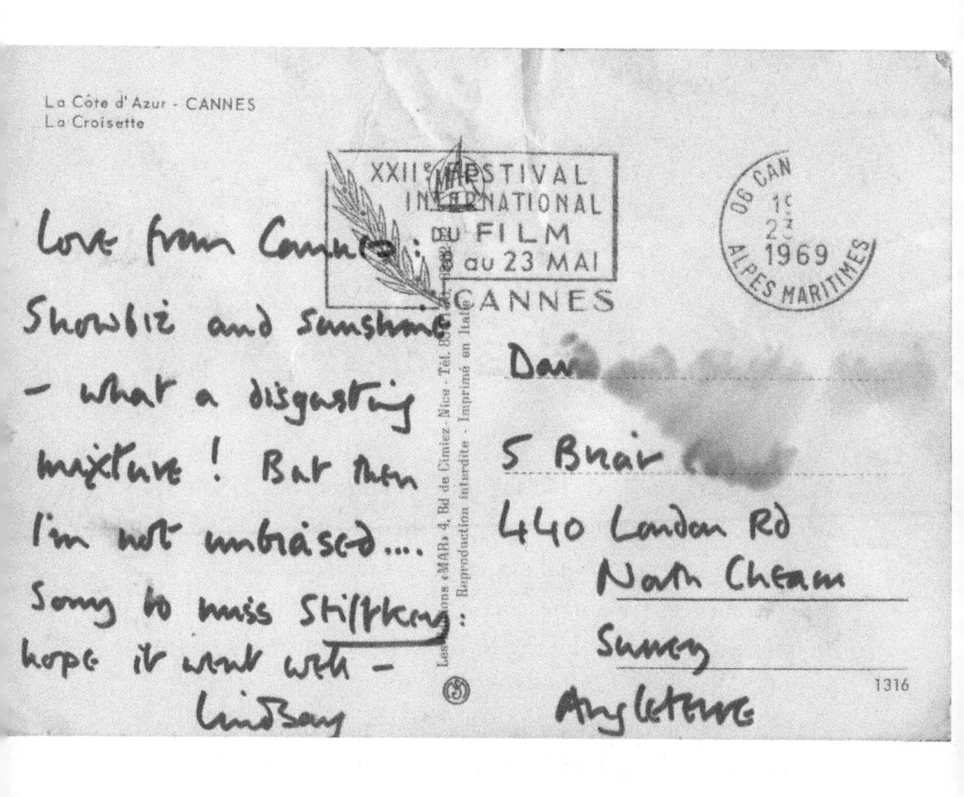

La Côte d'Azur - CANNES
La Croisette

XXIIe FESTIVAL INTERNATIONAL DU FILM
8 au 23 MAI
CANNES

06 CAN
1969
ALPES MARITIMES

Love from Cannes:
Showbiz and sunshine
– what a disgusting
mixture! But then
I'm not unbiased....
Sorry to miss Stiffkey
hope it went well –
Lindsay

Dan
5 Briar
440 London Rd
North Cheam
Surrey
Angleterre

1316

A postcard from Lindsay at Cannes, just before *If*.... won the Palme D'Or.

9

Fifty years on....

As usually happens, after filming *If....* we all went our various ways. Occasionally paths crossed, but not often. When they did – and occasionally still do – we all recognise and rejoice in the knowledge and memory that we were part of something rather special and unique that has stood the test of time. Fifty years later *If....* is as fresh and, I suspect, as relevant as ever.

Most of the older actors have now passed away, including Arthur Lowe, Mona Washbourne, Peter Jeffrey, Anthony Nicholls and Mary McLeod.

Graham Crowden, whom I so admired as an actor, and who was so brilliant as the history master, became a friend, an avuncular and much-respected lunch-companion, with whom I shared many happy conversations. His performance as *King Lear* at the Bristol Old Vic was quite brilliant, and his experience shone through one of his final performances in Agatha Christie's *And Then There Were None* in the West End. He introduced me to his actress daughter Sarah, who became another great friend. I last saw Graham, with his wife Phyllida, in Edinburgh, where they lived in retirement until his death in 2010. He had a full and rewarding career and life.

Sadly we have also lost some younger cast members, including Richard Warwick, whose life was cut short at the age of 52. Richard was a lovely man, with no vanity or pretentions. He was extremely good looking, with an endearing crinkly smile. He was a natural actor, who just appeared to do it with little effort. And yet there was great subtlety in his performance. He was something of a loner, in that he certainly never craved company, although he was always extremely friendly. A few years after *If*....he appeared in the BBC serial *The Last of the Mohicans*. Apparently, while filming in Scotland, he refused a room in the hotel where the film crew were based, and preferred to pitch a tent by the side of the river.

One story particularly reminds me of Richard's singular niceness. We were filming the study scenes at Merton Park Studios, and were allowed to have lunch, just the three of us, in the pub next door. We were all wearing our school uniform. The waitress came to take our order, and immediately expressed delighted astonishment at seeing Richard. 'Oh!' she exclaimed. 'My daughter will never believe this! She's your biggest fan!' She took our order and left the table. Richard was bemused. As far as he knew, there was no reason why the waitress's daughter would have known him. When she returned, again enthusing wildly, and bringing a piece of paper and a pen, asking him for an autograph, he took the bull by the horns and, with a lovely smile, asked her who she thought he was. The waitress laughed, as if Richard was sending her up. 'Paul Jones!' she said. 'My daughter loves your songs!' She hurried away, leaving the pen and paper. Paul Jones was a popular rhythm and blues singer with the Manfred Mann band. There was indeed a facial resemblance to Richard. 'What shall I do?' asked Richard. We discussed it. Either he should simply apologise for not being Paul Jones, or he could pretend that he was. In the end, Richard did the right thing. Knowing the disappointment he would cause if he didn't oblige, he simply signed the name 'Paul Jones' and graciously gave the autograph to the thrilled waitress, who hopefully never discovered the truth.

Christine Noonan died in 2003. She left us far too young too, at the age of 58. The last time I met her was on a tube train. She was teaching drama, and seemed very happy, although her acting career had clearly not been as successful as she would have liked. I can't help wondering if her bravely agreeing to do the nude café scene didn't hold back her progress. It must be remembered that in the '60s nudity on film was uncommon. Indeed, the scene in which Mrs Kemp, the Housemaster's Wife, walked naked through our dormitory, was nearly cut by the censor because her pubic hair was on view. He eventually allowed it to remain, in exchange for Lindsay agreeing to cut all the boys' genitalia visible in the shower scene. Lindsay had clearly thought ahead, because he had shot the shower scene in two ways, just in case. For Christine, I wonder whether she was right to agree to be filmed nude. Her career certainly didn't take off after the release of *If....* She was in an episode of the BBC's *Casanova*, in which Frank Finlay in the title role, sponged her, topless in a bath. In those days, perhaps actresses' reputations were somehow sullied by doing a nude scene. The year after her death, the British Film Institute organised a Lindsay Anderson tribute. His films were shown, and there were several interviews and discussions. Malcolm came over from America to take part in a question and answer session. There was a reception afterwards, where we met up for the first time for several years. Suddenly, into the room came a young woman. Malcolm and I stared in astonishment. For a moment we thought it was Christine. In fact, it was her daughter, who looked amazingly like her.

Robert Swann, who played Rowntree, died in 2006, aged sixty-one, having had a busy acting career on stage, in film and on television. He had, I discovered, a rather beautiful singing voice, and in 1973 agreed to appear with me in a musical revue I co-wrote called *Just the Ticket* at the Thorndike Theatre, Leatherhead. Robert had a great gift for comedy, too.

Peter Sproule, who played Barnes, another Whip, or prefect, also died too early, in 2010 aged 63. He appeared regularly on television and film, but it was his performance in Howard Brenton's notorious 1980 stage play, *The Romans in Britain,* that brought him most prominently into the spotlight. He and Greg Hicks were the National Theatre actors who played the male rape scene that led to the private prosecution for gross indecency brought by Mary Whitehouse.

Ben Aris, who endearingly played the hapless assistant master, subsequently became closely involved with my theatre productions. He was a very versatile actor, who could sing and dance really well. Later in the year we filmed *If....* (1968) he appeared in the revue *Three To One On*, along with John Gould and myself (the co-writers of the show) and Joyce Rae. The show toured and played a season at the Edinburgh Festival, from where it was picked up for a one-off 'special' on BBC2 television. Later, Ben played Professor Bosh in several productions of my musical play (co-written with Sheila Ruskin), *The Owl and the Pussycat Went to See...* He also played a zany Zookeeper in a tour of my musical play *Flibberty and the Penguin*, which was the pilot tour for Whirligig Theatre, the children's touring company I co-ran for twenty-five years. He was also a brilliant Red Admiral in the first London production of my musical play *The Plotters of Cabbage Patch Corner*, directed by Jonathan Lynn at the Shaw Theatre in 1971. Ben was another friend who died too soon, in 2003 at the age of sixty-three.

Others on Lindsay's team who are no longer with us include Neville Thompson, the genial Assistant to the Producers, who brought me my dummy script. He came back into my life several years later. In 1972 he was instrumental in arranging for me to be invited to write the screenplay of the Anglo-EMI/Theatre Projects feature film, *Swallows and Amazons*. He knew I had written several children's plays by that point, and suggested me to producer Richard Pilbrow. Neville worked on *Swallows* as Associate Producer and was a much-loved colleague. His quiet efficiency and mild manner must have endeared him to director Ken Russell, for whom he worked as Production Manager on many films, including *The Devils, The Music Lovers* and *The Boy Friend.* He also worked with members of the Monty Python team on *Time Bandits, The Missionary* and *Erik the Viking.* Neville died in 2002, aged sixty-eight.

Jocelyn Herbert, *If….*'s Production Designer, had previously worked mainly in theatre. She had a particularly fruitful relationship with the adventurous and experimental English Stage Company at the Royal Court Theatre, where she designed productions for George Devine, Lindsay, John Dexter and Tony Richardson, with whom she also collaborated on the film *Tom Jones.* After *If….*, Lindsay employed her on stage productions like John Arden's *Serjeant Musgrave's Dance* and David Storey's *Home* and *The Changing Room,* as well as on the films *O Lucky Man!* and *The Whales of August.* I met her several times while filming *If…..* She was always friendly and found time to chat. We had a brief, warm reunion in 2002 when we both attended *If….*'s second premiére at the Curzon in Shaftesbury Avenue. The British Film Institute re-released it with a new print. Back in 1970, Jocelyn unwittingly played a role in one of my most embarrassing experiences. It was the first night of David Mercer's *After Haggerty*, in which I was playing Roger for the Royal Shakespeare Company at the Aldwych Theatre. After the performance I was washing and changing in my dressing room when there was a knock on the door. In popped an elderly lady, who proceeded to talk about the play and ask questions about the performance. Irritated by this interruption from an eccentric, who I imagined was always barging into actors' dressing rooms or hanging around stage doors, I behaved rather rudely, answering brusquely, and getting on with my ablutions in readiness for a visit from my guests. Eventually the lady left. But later, as I set off for the first night party, I saw her again, standing near the stage door with …… Jocelyn Herbert. We greeted each other warmly, then Jocelyn turned to her companion. 'David,' she said. 'Have you met Dame Peggy?' I blushed with shame as Dame Peggy

February 21st 2002 (my birthday!), when the BFI released a new print of *If....* and we had a second premiere at the Curzon, Soho. Left to right: Rupert Webster (Bobby Phillips), Philip Bagenal (Peanuts), Charles Sturridge (Markland), ? , Jocelyn Herbert, Michael Medwin (Producer), David Sherwin (Writer), Kathy Burke, Lois Smith, Mary MacLeod (Mrs Kemp), David Wood (Johnny)

Ashcroft, one of our greatest actresses, smiled and graciously shook my hand. Jocelyn continued to design for film and theatre, including at the National Theatre and the Royal Shakespeare Company, almost until her death in 2003 aged eighty-six.

David Sherwin continued to work with Lindsay, writing the screenplays for *O Lucky Man!* and *Britannia Hospital.* For John Schlesinger he worked on *Sunday Bloody Sunday* (1971). In 1996 he published a memoir, *Going Mad in Hollywood: And Life with Lindsay Anderson*, in which he described the trials and tribulations of his screenwriting attempts in America, his struggle with depression, and his friendship and working relationship with Lindsay. Sadly David died in January, 2018, aged 75.

In 2006 at Riverside Studios, Hammersmith, I was reunited with Miroslav 'Mirek' Ondricek at a festival celebrating his cinematography organised by Czech Central London. Together with Stephen Frears we took part in a panel discussion about *If....* chaired by Paul Ryan. Lindsay had met Mirek at the Karlovy Vary Film Festival, where he had been showing *This Sporting Life.* Mirek was filming *A Blonde in Love* for Milos Forman. In the following years Mirek continued to work for Forman on films like *Ragtime, Hair* and *Amadeus.* He returned to the UK to work with Lindsay and Malcolm on *O Lucky Man!* He died in 2015, aged eighty. I shall always remember his quiet authority on the set as he huddled with Lindsay and Jirina, the Czech interpreter, discussing the next shot.

Those of the *If....* family who have survived fifty years since the film was made include our producers Michael Medwin and Albert Finney, whose company Memorial Enterprises produced other films, including *Spring and Port Wine, Gumshoe (*Stephen Frears' first feature) and Lindsay's *O Lucky Man!.* I last met Albert when he was co-starring with Rachel Roberts in Ted Whitehead's play *Alpha Beta* at the Royal Court Theatre. It was my pleasure to escort Shelley Winters, with whom I had been acting in a two-hander play for London Weekend Television called *The Vamp.* She had met

Albert in America, so we were invited to his dressing room after the play, along with another visiting movie star, Kirk Douglas. I last saw Michael when I was directing my play *Babe, the Sheep-Pig* at Regent's Park Open Air Theatre in 2006. Michael was playing a 'rude mechanical' in the concurrent production of *A Midsummer Night's Dream,* at the age of eighty-three. We often exchanged *If....* reminiscences.

Tim Van Rellim, the second assistant director, who spent time chatting to me on the roof of Cheltenham College Chapel, became a successful film producer. His recent credits include *A Knight's Tale* (2001*), Dragonball: Evolution* and *Salmon Fishing in the Yemen* (2011).

Stephen Frears, *If....*'s third assistant director, who checked our costumes at a daily roll call, subsequently became a significant director in his own right. First, he directed for television. He worked for the BBC on *Play for Today* and was reunited with Lindsay on Alan Bennett's *The Old Crowd* for London Weekend Television; Lindsay directed the actors and Stephen directed in the gallery. Since then he has directed highly successful feature films including *Gumshoe* (1971), *My Beautiful Laundrette* (1985), *Prick Up Your Ears* (1987), *Dangerous Liaisons* (1988), *Philomena* (2013) and *Victoria and Abdul* (2017). He received Oscar nominations for Best Director for *The Grifters (*1990) and *The Queen* (2006).

Stuart Baird, the other assistant director, who brought us whisky before we shot the 'nail in the head' scene, later became a leading film editor, particularly of action films, including *Lethal Weapon, Gorillas in the Mist, Die Hard 2, Casino Royale* and *Skyfall.* He worked a lot with director Richard Donner, on films like *Superman,* for which he received an Oscar nomination for Best Film Editing. Stuart has also successfully directed several feature films, including *Star Trek: Nemesis.*

Of the older actors, to my knowledge only Geoffrey Chater, who so skilfully played the questionable Chaplain, remains with us at the age of ninety-four. I remember him as a charming gentleman, who was uncomfortable about tweaking new boy Jute's nipple. He was probably uncomfortable in the Headmaster's drawer too!

Some of my fellow schoolboys in *If....* have, fifty years later, been impossible to trace, some have continued to work in the world of entertainment, some have changed careers.

Prefects Michael Cadman (Fortinbras) and Hugh Thomas (Denson) carried on acting, though Hugh first went to Oxford University. Michael appeared in the film *Twisted Nerve* and television programmes including *Poldark, Emmerdale* and *Cadfael.* Hugh appeared in several TV series in his native Wales, including *Pobol y Cym, High Hopes* and *Satellite City,* and films including *The Tall Guy* and *Breaking Glass.* He also co-wrote with Christopher Tookey the musical adaptation of Dickens' *Hard Times* that I much enjoyed at the Theatre Royal, Haymarket in 2000. The show had started life as an Oxford student production, directed by Charles Sturridge, who had also appeared in *If....* as the junior, Markland.

Of we senior boys, Malcolm has, of course, had most success as an actor. For fifty years he has rarely been off the big screen, from *A Clockwork Orange* (1971) to *The Artist* (2011). And he has had recurring roles in numerous TV series such as *Heroes, Franklin and Bash* and *Mozart in the Jungle.* He never stops. All power to his elbow. He thoroughly deserves his star on the Hollywood Walk of Fame.

Robin Askwith (Keating) starred in the racy *Confessions* films and has been seen on television in *Coronation Street* and *Benidorm.* On stage he has acted in many plays and pantomimes.

David Griffin (Willens) was a regular in TV series *Hi-de-Hi!* and *Keeping Up Appearances.* He has also appeared on stage in plays and pantomimes.

Richard Everett (Pussy Graves) has had a varied career. He continued acting into the 1980s, and has written several successful stage plays, including *Entertaining Angels,* which starred Penelope Keith and continues to be played regularly. Richard has also written many animation scripts including *Timbuctoo* and *Nellie the Elephant,* and given drama workshops. He also co-produced the film *Two Men Went to War* (2002). Richard and I have met quite recently, because we share the same literary agency.

Philip Bagenal (Peanuts) and Robert Yetzes (Fisher) have found success outside acting. Philip co-founded, designed and ran the very successful Eastcote Studios, a recording studio in West London. Star names from Duran Duran to Adele, Depeche Mode to Arctic Monkeys, Tom Jones to Pixie Lott have recorded their hits here. Bob, whose character memorably stole an extra bun at breaktime, is now Chief Executive Officer of Bryn Melyn Care, in Shropshire, a residential care home that transforms the lives of vulnerable young people. He remembers asking Lindsay why his lines had been cut. Lindsay replied that 'someone out there is a snitch and told Michael Medwin you are not a member of Equity. I had no choice, but your day will come', a clever yet confusing explanation for a sixteen-year-old.

Of the Junior boys, Charles Sturridge (Markland) has achieved much. In *If....* he had a memorable scene in which, amidst the chaos of the Sweat Room, he carefully unwrapped peaches from his trunk. He became a very successful television director, cutting his teeth on the brilliant *Brideshead Revisited* in 1981. Out of the blue in 1999 he invited me to play a cameo role in his Channel 4 epic adaptation of Dava Sobel's *Longitude.* I had a thoroughly enjoyable two days filming with Michael Gambon and John Wood. In 2002 he directed the acclaimed *Shackleton*. Charles married Phoebe Nicholls, daughter of Anthony 'General Denson' Nicholls. One of their children is actor Tom Sturridge.

Brian Pettifer, who played the hapless Biles, whose head is ignominiously pushed down a lavatory, has acted ever since *If....* He worked for Lindsay again in *O Lucky Man!* and *Britannia Hospital* and also appeared in *Amadeus* and many television programmes and series. He also writes and directs for the theatre, and in 2017 opened in a new play called *Yer Granny* at the Kings Theatre, Glasgow.

Rupert Webster (Bobby Phillips) never appeared in front of the camera again, having beautifully portrayed the young admirer of Wallace, watching him perform gymnastics and later seen sharing his bed. Many of us, including Lindsay, believed a rumour that he had died young, but later we discovered he had been in America for several years, where he studied art and played guitar in several rock bands. In 2002 he attended the Gala Screening of the refurbished print of *If….* at the Curzon, Shaftesbury Avenue, looking as fresh and handsome as ever, if a little older.

Robin Davies, whose character Machin held sway over the Juniors' Sweat Room, continued acting until his untimely death from cancer in 2010 at the age of fifty-six. He was perhaps best remembered for playing Carrot in the television series *Catweazle*, as well as appearing in *And Mother Makes Three.* His film appearances included *Blood on Satan's Claw* and *Shakespeare in Love.* He was also in Lindsay's *Britannia Hospital.*

Martin Beaumont (Hunter) has been in show business all his life. In 1968, as well as *If….* he appeared in *Chitty Chitty Bang Bang* and *Oliver!* A love of comedy developed from working, in his teens, with Morecambe and Wise and Les Dawson. He became a stand-up comic, winning the *Time Out* Comic of the Year Award. He writes, teaches, still acts on television and in commercials, and has worked as a comedy magician.

Michael Newport (Brunning) and Sean Bury (Jute) were brilliant, along with Charles Sturridge (Markland), in the scene in which Jute, the new boy, is ruthlessly quizzed about school slang expressions and their meanings. Michael was in *Mischief* in 1969. He had earlier played a Newspaper Boy in *Life At The Top.* But he appears to have stopped acting by the end of the seventies. Sean continued acting in films, including *The Abominable Dr Phibes* and two films directed by Lewis Gilbert, *Friends* (1971) and *Paul and Michelle* (1974). He also appeared on television in *The Onedin Line* and one-off plays. His last film role was, I think, in *The Spy Who Loved Me* (1977). An undated article in the Brighton College Old Boys newsletter tells us that Sean changed careers. '*I now work with people with special needs,'* he writes. '*The money is terrible but the smiles are the best! I have been lucky enough to see both of these two very different worlds. One feeds upon the attention it seeks and the other is just happy being, and getting on with things quietly, but both are exciting, fun and challenge one to do better.'*

POSTSCRIPT

In 1972 my agent received a phone call checking my availability for another Lindsay Anderson film, to also star Malcolm McDowell, called *O Lucky Man!* My immediate instinct, of course, was to tell my agent to reply that, whatever I was doing, I would somehow make myself free to work again with Lindsay. Indeed I was having a busy year. I played opposite Shelley Winters in a two-hander play for London Weekend television called *The Vamp*. On stage I went to Toronto, playing opposite Sir Michael Redgrave in John Mortimer's play *A Voyage Round My Father*. I had two children's plays coming into London for Christmas, *The Owl and the Pussycat Went to See…* and *The Plotters of Cabbage Patch Corner*, and I was writing another, *The Papertown Paperchase*, for the Swan Theatre, Worcester. But I was determined not to have to turn down another job with Lindsay and his team. Sadly it was not to be. We didn't get a call back. I was never offered a role in the film. And I never had the invitation to work with him again.

However, in the early 1990s there were rumours that Lindsay was planning a sequel to *If….*, in which several of the characters would be reunited some thirty years on. Malcolm rang me a couple of times from America to say that David Sherwin and Lindsay were working on the script. Apparently the film was to take place back at the school, on Founders' Day. Mick Travis has become an Oscar-nominated movie star, who has left England for Hollywood. Wallace has risen through the army ranks to become a major who has lost an arm. Johnny, my character, is now a clergyman. It seems that Rowntree, the former Head of School who gave us a beating, is kidnapped by a group of anti-war students and saved by Mick, Johnny and Wallace, but not before Mick manages to crucify Rowntree with a long nail through his palm. I never saw a script, but sadly Lindsay died in 1994, so the project was abandoned. He had a heart attack while swimming in France. He was seventy-one.

Now, nearly fifty years after making *If....* the film still features regularly in my daily life. Movie buffs send messages to my website, asking questions or simply saying how important seeing *If.....* was in their formative years. For some time after the première in 1969 I was recognised, including once in a supermarket in Toronto! Not long ago, at a funeral, a man in his sixties, realising who I was, invited me to play scenes from *If....* with him – he knew all the lines! And, I understand, film students study *If....*, so each new generation appreciates and gives it critical attention. The film still resonates with young people, who understand how little Britain has changed in the last fifty years, in terms of its hierarchical class structure. Public school life may be gentler, but, as a metaphor for our national life, *If....* is still, I believe, relevant. And it remains as living testament to Lindsay's genius. For me, acting in *If....* was a major feature not only on my CV but also of my life.

AFTERWORD

Remembering Lindsay

by George Perry

Meeting Lindsay Anderson was always a challenging experience, no matter how well you knew him. Would he be irascible or genial? Would he greet you as a friend or treat you with disdain? Would he trap you into saying something foolish and then apply cold logic to ridicule you? You never quite knew what to expect and it was best to be prepared for the worst. You could be sure of an enlivening and exciting time, a stimulating encounter with a formidable intelligence. He was apt to probe and test in a donnish way, rather as though it were an Oxbridge tutorial. His rare acting appearance in *Chariots of Fire*, as the head of a Cambridge college, was the most apt of typecasting. He expected your assertions to be backed by proof. "Why do you say that?" he would ask. He loved to engage in dialectics, especially where his work was concerned. You had to be careful when you praised him. Unless you showed some depth of perception he would dismiss you. "You're not being sincere."

As a journalist on a quality Sunday broadsheet I knew him for many years. He was never aloof or inaccessible, and would often telephone or write if something appeared that met with his disapproval. He despised newspaper proprietors with more opprobrium than their unfortunate hacks, and regarded us as apparatchiks in an ignoble cause Some of my critical colleagues found his combativeness tiresome and boring, particularly if they were placed on the defensive, as was usually the case. I forgave his uncompromising stance. I recognised that he was an original artistic thinker, and felt that knowing him was a privilege.

I had first read his critical writings when I was a Cambridge undergraduate in the mid-1950s. For me 1956 was not just the year of Suez and the failed Hungarian revolution, but the creative explosion of what the press called "The Angry Young Men". The Royal Court Theatre may have been the site of the main action, but Lindsay Anderson was in the vanguard with his influential polemical essay in *Sight and Sound*, "Stand Up! Stand Up!" which poleaxed contemporary critical thinking and demanded an acceptance of responsibility from film-makers and the commentating media to jolt an indifferent public into awareness of the importance of film. His buzzword was 'commitment', a repudiation of the lazy, philistine pursuit of meretricious values, and a call for boldness and conviction. By then he was already securing a name beyond his writing as a maker of documentaries, mainly financed by sponsorship. He sought to find the poetry in common humanity, and his work was impressive. One of his films, *Thursday's Children*, about a school for the deaf and dumb, had won an Oscar, although typically he deplored the self-serving smugness of the Academy that had presented the award.

Although a stir was generated by his impassioned call, there was no seismic shift in attitudes. There was a brief flowering of a British new wave as the 1960s loomed. With films such as Tony Richardson's *A Taste of Honey* and *The Loneliness of the Long Distance Runner*, Karel Reisz's *Saturday Night and Sunday Morning*, and Jack

Clayton's *Room at the Top* – all adapted from works by provincial, mainly northern writers – a new dawn seemed possible.

As it happened, Lindsay Anderson's feature debut in 1963, the gritty study of a flawed hero and a failed relationship, *This Sporting Life*, in collaboration with the novelist and playwright David Storey, was arguably the best of the bunch, but after its box-office failure it lowered the curtain on a short-lived movement. Sir John Davis, the pragmatic accountant who ran the Rank Organisation which had backed the film, bitterly rued that decision made against his better judgment. Finding myself next to him at a dinner not long after, I remember him raging at it as squalid kitchen-sink stuff, and adding that his sort of film was *The Chalk Garden*, with Hayley Mills and a U certificate.

Lindsay had a fearsome reputation for not suffering fools, whether it was gladly or mostly otherwise. The sad truth was that the necessity to suffer fools dictated much of his creative life. Particularly in the world of cinema, where the fools ruled.

It is why his legacy is only a handful of feature films. Projects came to nothing because of his uncompromising, obdurate attitude. Yet all of those that did achieve fruition are remarkable, from the harsh world of a league rugby player, *This Sporting Life*, through *If....*, *O Lucky Man!* and *Britannia Hospital*, the three films that comprised the loose, iconoclastic, bile-laden trilogy attacking his perceived dystopia of contemporary Britain, with Malcolm McDowell as the protagonist.

His sole American feature, *The Whales of August*, was a gentler elegiac piece uniting two legendary screen actresses, Lillian Gish and Bette Davis, in their twilight. It was an extraordinary undertaking that in the making was fraught with peril. "Directing Bette Davis," he said after her death, "was like playing with a very sharp knife."

Sparse as his film output was, it should be remembered that he also scaled great artistic heights in theatre, particularly during his reign with the English Stage Company. Somewhere I still have the Royal Court programme for *The Lily White Boys* with Albert Finney, in which he describes himself as an ex-critic and an ex-film director. That was in 1960, with several film documentaries behind him and as yet, no features to his name. It is rare but not unique for directors to excel in both film and stage and, but for his passion for cinema and persistence, Lindsay could have stuck with theatre and possibly a few forays into television.

Not to be overlooked are his several notable books, including his compendious, monumental and unsurpassed study of John Ford. As a critic and essayist his words still resonate and reward whoever seeks them out today. Early on he sought the role of cultural rebel and made it his calling, almost out of a sense of duty to art. He always regarded film as the perfect outlet for the bile that had begun to bubble within when he was at public school, which just happened to be Cheltenham, later the principal location for *If....*

His background was unusual for someone striving for a career in such a precarious, raffish business as film-making. He was Scottish, and it showed in his craggy, firm-jawed, thin-lipped features and keen eyes that hinted of heather and Highland gusts, the look of a laird rather than a ghillie. His father was an army general, his mother came from the Bell whisky clan. He was born in Bangalore in 1923, a scion of the Raj. After Cheltenham he went up to Wadham College, Oxford as a classicist, but the war intervened. He served in the King's Rifles and the Intelligence Corps, and in July 1945 risked the wrath of his colonel by contriving to fly a red flag over the Delhi officers' mess to celebrate the Labour victory at Westminster.

Back at Wadham he switched to English, and by now convinced in the potency of film to transmit radical ideas, became an element of an intriguing group that included Tony Richardson, Gavin Lambert, Penelope Houston and later Karel Reisz who had been at Cambridge. They produced a magazine, first in Oxford then London, called *Sequence*, which uniquely, in a time when audiences had never been bigger yet more non-discriminating, discussed cinema intelligently and critically. In those early post-war days, film-going was the prime national pastime, cinemas dominated every high street, and television was still embryonic. Films may have been abundant, but distribution and exhibition were rigidly controlled by Hollywood and a duopoly of circuits controlled by Rank and ABC imposed strict limits on what was shown. Beyond the rarefied London arthouses - the Academy and Studio One in Oxford Street and the Curzon in Mayfair - foreign films had little or no exposure, and brave as *Sequence* was, it collapsed after fourteen issues. Lambert and Houston went off to transform *Sight and Sound*, the then dismal journal of the British Film Institute. Lambert soon departed to Hollywood and a career as screenwriter, novelist and biographer, leaving Houston to edit it for thirty-five years, and providing a regular critical platform for Lindsay Anderson. He, Richardson and Reisz, joined by the cinematographer Walter Lassally, then founded Free Cinema, a documentary movement that distanced itself from the John Grierson and Crown Film Unit tradition and strived for realism and authenticity.

Talent is only part of the requisite for making progress in the film industry and making the second feature is probably a greater challenge than the first, especially if the box-office yield has not matched the critical reception. A highly-regarded young film director, who died before he could confirm his success, once said to me that directing was "five per cent filming, ninety-five per cent hustling", by which he meant that the battle to get a film off the ground occupied far more time than that of physically making it.

It took another five years for Lindsay Anderson to start his next film which was to be *If....*, and it went through many metamorphoses after David Sherwin's original idea had surfaced. It was turned down by every British production house in spite of all best efforts. Then Paramount, assured by the persuasive charm of Michael Medwin, Lindsay's producer, rescued it and gave the green light. Which is why Lindsay would often say that it was an American picture.

Allegedly Paramount was dismayed by the finished film and only released it to fill the slot left by *Barbarella*, an expensive flop. They were rewarded in spite of their loss of faith. *If….* had already won the Palme d'Or at Cannes and elicited many favourable reviews, as well as outrage from those who felt it disgraced Britain. The public nevertheless went for it and it was a box-office hit. Events had helped. The year of release, 1968, was marked by waves of violent protest across the world. France was paralysed by ten million strikers and Paris and Berlin erupted in student uprisings. Civil rights and anti-Vietnam riots engulfed the United States. The Prague Spring blossomed in Czechoslovakia, quickly followed by its brutal Russian suppression. Grosvenor Square in London was the scene of vicious fighting between protestors and police.

The notion of a staid, hidebound institution, an English public school that had been coasting on centuries of tradition and was now suddenly blown apart by bloody revolution and reckoning, struck chords wholly appropriate to the prevailing zeitgeist.

There were three predominant influences on Lindsay Anderson's cinematic creativity. First was the British documentarist, Humphrey Jennings, whose sense of poetic realism separated him from his contemporaries, and whose wartime propaganda shorts such as *Words for Battle*, *Listen to Britain* and *A Diary for Timothy* were miniature masterpieces of editing.

Then there was the prolific, long-lived giant of Hollywood, John Ford, who he idolised for his mastery of story-telling, lyrical sense of the epic sweep of American history and instinctive skill in the mission of hanging a film together. He knew Ford well and had many discussions with him, as well as writing his definitive study, *About John Ford*. Strangely, only when Ford was dying, and he visited him at his home in Palm Desert, did he get around to calling him "Jack" instead of "Mr Ford" or "Sir".

Lastly, there was Jean Vigo, who died in 1934 at the age of twenty-nine, having made only four films, two of which are undeniably masterworks. Lindsay asked his production team to watch Vigo's *Zéro de Conduite* (Nought for Conduct) in which rebellious French schoolboys trapped in a rigid, bureaucratic educational institution destroy the place and crush the staff in an anarchic, surreal explosion of uncontrolled rage and joy. It was a mood-setter for Lindsay's own vision of a school as a metaphor for a complacent, yet fundamentally dysfunctional British Establishment.

He believed greatly in the value of appropriate casting, and while Malcolm McDowell and Christine Noonan were almost immediately recognised as good fits, he took immense care in selecting the other Crusaders, the rebels against the system, as David Wood describes in his memoir. For his small parts he strived to use actors with strong personalities who could bring depth to their characters. Graham Crowden, Peter Jeffrey, Mona Washbourne and Arthur Lowe were among the many who illuminated the acting quality.

The school is a disturbing, nasty place, an engine of conformity where the sycophants and bullies flourish, and the mavericks are treated as deviants and outcasts. It is how most public schools behaved then, although perhaps less extremely. David Sherwin bitterly remembered his own experiences at Tonbridge. Cheltenham College was sent a doctored script and on its basis granted use of its premises as a location, expecting perhaps a benign updating of *Goodbye Mr Chips*. It is now co-educational, and its website makes no mention of Lindsay Anderson as a distinguished alumnus.

British cinema is the better for having him, even though he is now a generally-forgotten figure of the mid-twentieth century. He resented that the fine French director, Francois Truffaut, who had also been greatly influenced by Jean Vigo when he made his first feature *Les Quatre Cents Coups* (The 400 Blows) declared the term "British cinema" to be an oxymoron. A harsh condemnation, but Lindsay admitted that he found much of it to be anaemic and genteel, anodyne and self-satisfied.

Even the greatly-admired output of Michael Balcon's Ealing

Studios was to his eye often cosy and suburban. He recognised the achievements of Michael Powell and Emeric Pressburger, creators of *A Matter of Life and Death* and *The Red Shoes*, in breaking the mould and deplored the former's neglect by the industry when the partnership ended. He could not understand why Carol Reed could make three outstanding films in a row (*Odd Man Out*, *The Fallen Idol*, *The Third Man*) then descend into mediocrity. He celebrated the David Lean of *Brief Encounter*, *Great Expectations* and *Oliver Twist*, but relegated him in his later career for succumbing to commercial Hollywood and mega-budgets. He felt that the superbly-accomplished Alfred Hitchcock lost much former integrity when he forged a new career in California and he claimed, in opposition to critical voices (particularly in France), that he was not a serious director.

A typically contrarian position. But then it was his nature to run against the tide. He had so many contradictory positions. Although an instinctive man of the left, he did not like to be called a socialist. He found Labour governments dirigiste and bureaucratic, and was saddened by trade unions obsessed with restrictive practices and preservation of the status quo. He hated to be called an intellectual, yet devoted more mental effort to fomenting ideas and understanding than most of his peers.

There was no tradition in Britain for critics to become film-makers, unlike in France where a clutch of them, including Godard, Truffaut, Chabrol, Rohmer and Rivette, migrated from the pages of *Cahiers du Cinéma* to the director's chair. Far, however, from identifying with them, he scorned their arid adherence to intellectualism, particularly the 'auteur theory' which ascribed absolutely everything that happened on film to its director. He recognised that a finished film was the consequence of a synergic culmination of a multitude of talents, that the process of filming was often haphazard and arbitrary, with the director at the mercy of circumstance. Unlike Hitchcock who revelled, often in amusement, to academic theorising of his work, Lindsay abhorred film studies courses and regarded practical experience as the best way to learn a craft.

Part of the anger that drove him undoubtedly derived from his repressed homosexuality. He was not 'outed' until after his death, by Gavin Lambert. He had many friends, but always preserved privacy and loyalty. There is no reason to suppose that he was anything but celibate. There were women in his life. The actresses Rachel Roberts, who had co-starred with Richard Harris in *This Sporting Life*, and Jill Bennett were devoted to him. Helen Mirren said she loved him and called him "the pepper in the arse of the Establishment." Malcolm McDowell, who became his protégé as he steered him through the trilogy of Mick Travis films and induced Stanley Kubrick to cast him as the lead in *A Clockwork Orange*, was perfectly aware that Lindsay was fixated on him. Also that he had been drawn unrequitedly to other heterosexual leading men, including Richard Harris who he ennobled like a Greek hero in the brutal rugby league encounters in *This Sporting Life*, and Albert Finney who he had directed on stage. It was as though he was attracted to them because they were unattainable. Long before Lambert - an active homosexual - spilled the beans in his book *Mainly About Lindsay Anderson*, it was commonly known in film and theatre circles that Lindsay was gay, but in that tolerant environment it was never particularly an issue.

My last memory of him was in 1994. I was presenting a radio arts programme on British documentaries of the 1930s and 1940s. There could be only one person properly qualified to talk about Humphrey Jennings and that was Lindsay Anderson. He eagerly responded to the invitation. I was careful to warn the team in advance, especially the young women production assistants, that he was likely to be brusque and curmudgeonly, would expect his taxi to Broadcasting House to arrive on the dot and would require a deferential welcome.

When Lindsay made his entrance he breezed in, smiling graciously at everyone, and then embarked on an exemplary interview in which he explained the significance of Humphrey Jennings, accepting that ninety-five per cent of the listeners would not have heard of him, and making his case without a hint of patronage or superiority. It was a stunning display of professionalism. When the recording had finished, he lingered over tea and BBC biscuits, talking to the girls with avuncular charm and delighting all with his anecdotage and insights, until eventually the producer, mindful of precious studio time and his taxi clocking up the waiting minutes, had to move him on. I felt a surge of warmth and affection for the old tiger as he went away happy, leaving me to explain to the bemused staff that somehow he must have mellowed.

It was possibly his last broadcast. Shortly afterwards he went to France and died.

With thanks to Paramount for allowing me to use on-camera and off-camera photographs.